YEARS WITH FRANK LLOYD WRIGHT

APPRENTICE TO GENIUS

EDGAR TAFEL

DOVER PUBLICATIONS, INC., NEW YORK

Published in Canada by General Publishing Company, Ltd., 30 Lesmill Road, Don Mills, Toronto, Ontario.
Published in the United Kingdom by Constable and Company, Ltd.

This Dover edition, first published in 1985, is an unabridged republication of the work first published in 1979 by McGraw-Hill Book Company, New York, under the title *Apprentice to Genius: Years with Frank Lloyd Wright*. Illustrations on pp. 4–6, 56–62, 87–90, 155–158, 207, 210, 214–218, originally in color, are here reproduced in black and white.

Manufactured in the United States of America
Dover Publications, Inc., 31 East 2nd Street, Mineola, N.Y. 11501

Library of Congress Cataloging in Publication Data

Tafel, Edgar.
  Years with Frank Lloyd Wright.

  Reprint. Originally published: Apprentice to genius. New York : McGraw-Hill, 1979.
  Includes index.
  1. Tafel, Edgar.   2. Architects—United States—Biography.   3. Wright, Frank Lloyd, 1867-1959.   I. Title.
NA737.W7A2   1985   720′.92′4 [B]   84-21210
ISBN 0-486-24801-1

CONTENTS

PREFACE

All during my architectural practice, people have asked how I met Frank Lloyd Wright, how long I worked for him, why I finally left, what life at Taliesin was like, what subsequent relationship I had with him until his death in 1959. "What was it like to work under the fury and wrath of genius?" they have asked. "What was he really like?" "Weren't you afraid of losing your identity?"

During my nine years of apprenticeship, from 1932 to 1941, and in later years, I took photographs of Mr. Wright's buildings during and after construction. The pictures were not arranged into a continuous slide message until the early 1970s, when the United States Information Agency (USIA) made it possible for me to lecture in Israel, England, and India. Interest in Frank Lloyd Wright in Liverpool, Jerusalem, Madras, and other places I visited was startling, considering how little was known there of his power and creative individuality.

It is a fact that modern architecture was born, bred, and brought up in our own Midwest and that finally only Mr. Wright's persistence took this development to Europe. He accomplished this first by having his organic buildings built and second by having material about his work published in Europe in 1910 and 1925. European publications alone brought serious notice of his work to America. Mr. Wright's force helped eradicate some two hundred years of formal architectural Beaux-Arts traditional "looking backward" training. Most Europeans erroneously still think the modern movement started with them.

In the States I was asked to lecture, as Mr. Wright had done, not often in the hallowed halls of the architectural establishment, but wherever new ideas were sought. Colleagues, friends, and employees then suggested that I write a book about my experiences with Mr. Wright. I did not take the idea seriously until Jeremy Robinson of McGraw-Hill appeared and persuaded me.

Mrs. Olgivanna Lloyd Wright graciously gave her blessing, offered her creative advice, and permitted the use of letters. Cariolana Simon stayed with the project a long time, putting my cryptic notes into context, and along with her valued creative research and writing, she devoted her total enthusiasm to the preparation of the basic manuscript. William Massee, friend, sometime client, writer, urged me to complete the work, by means of cajolery, editing, flattery, and extended help. Ben Raeburn of Horizon Press first suggested the book. Esther Gelatt edited and valiantly battled my trivia, and my staff weathered my seemingly endless "important" passages. Pedro Guerrero, former Taliesin photographer, gave freely of his great photos and help. Al Krescanko generously furnished his photos of Mr. Wright in the drafting room and at the Johnson Building. Herbert and Katherine Jacobs, friends and Wright clients, gave photographs and encouragement. Jan White, sensitive to history, sensitive to the topic and the available material, was an inspiration to work with in the book's design and visual editing. Edgar Kaufmann, ex-apprentice, historian, longtime friend, and delightful perfectionist, offered valuable advice and suggestions—all of which I took.

Mr. Wright is my fondest exemplar, and without him and his loyal apprentices there would be no story.

Edgar Tafel

1

Fall, 1935. Taliesin, Wisconsin: "Come along, E.J. We're ready for you," boomed Mr. Wright into the hand-cranked telephone. The call was from Pittsburgh and E.J. was Edgar J. Kaufmann, Sr., department store president. Mr. Wright was to show him the first sketches for his new house, "Fallingwater."

I looked across my drafting table at the apprentice in front of me, Bob Mosher, whose back had stiffened at the words. Ready? There wasn't one line drawn.

Kaufmann, an important client, coming to see plans for his house, and was Mr. Wright still carrying the design confidently around in his head?

Their relationship had started in a discussion one Sunday evening the year before when Mr. and Mrs. Kaufmann came out to visit their son, also an apprentice. Sunday evening in the living room at Taliesin was our weekly social event, all in formal dress. There was homemade wine, dinner cooked and served by apprentices, then music—piano, violin, solos, chorus. This evening ended with Mr. Wright's words of gratitude for our culinary labors and his general philosophical comments. Sitting back in his accustomed chair and addressing his remarks to the group, but

Top: Apprentices gathered around Broadacre City model at La Hacienda, our temporary Arizona headquarters.
Bottom: Apprentices working on details.

his message to the potential client, he expanded his theory for the salvation of America—his vision of the future city based on the automobile, Broadacre City. Mr. Wright declared that if he could, he would create an exhibit of models and drawings of Broadacres and send the message all over the United States. E.J. asked, "What would it take to produce such an exhibit?" Mr. Wright replied without hesitation, "$1000." E.J.: "Mr. Wright, you can start tomorrow." We started tomorrow.

The exhibit was made that winter, our first in Arizona. In the spring four of us apprentices trucked it across the country and through a Kansas dust storm to an exhibit in Rockefeller Center, which then toured the country. That summer Kaufmann commissioned Mr. Wright to design his country house.

Mr. Wright visited the site to help select the appropriate spot on a 2000-acre piece of family land 60 miles south of Pittsburgh—there were fields, gulches, ravines, hillslopes wooded and bare. After much walking, according to Mr. Wright, he asked, "E.J., where do you like to sit?" And E.J. pointed to a massive rock whose crest commanded a view over a waterfall and down into a glen. That spot, Mr. Kaufmann's stone seat, was to become the heart and hearthstone of the most famous house of the twentieth century.

So that morning in the drafting room, when we overheard him bellow, "Come along, E.J.," we wondered what could happen. Kaufmann, calling from Pittsburgh, was planning to drive to Chicago, then to Milwaukee, and come to Taliesin. It was the morning that Kaufmann called again from Milwaukee, 140 miles away from Spring Green, and only 140 minutes of driving at a mile a minute, that Mr. Wright was to start drawing. Kaufmann was en route.

He hung up the phone, briskly emerged from his office, some twelve steps from the drafting room, sat down at the table set with the plot plan, and started to draw. First floor plan. Second floor. Section, elevation. Side sketches of details, talking *sotto voce* all the while. The design just poured out of him. "Liliane and E.J. will have tea on the balcony . . . they'll cross the bridge to walk into the woods . . ." Pencils being used up as fast as we could sharpen them when broken—H's, HB's, colored Castell's, again and again being worn down or broken. Erasures, overdrawing, modifying. Flipping sheets back and forth. Then, the bold title across the bottom: "Fallingwater." A house has to have a name. . . .

Just before noon Mr. Kaufmann arrived. As he walked up the outside stone steps, he was greeted graciously by the master. They came straight to the drafting table. "E.J.," said Mr. Wright, "we've been waiting for you." The description of the house, its setting, philosophy, poured out. Poetry in form, line, color, textures and materials, all for a greater glory: a reality to live in! Mr. Wright at his eloquent and romantic best—he had done it before and would often do it again—genius through an organic growth along with nature. Kaufmann nodded in affirmation.

They went up to the hill garden dining room for lunch, and while they were away Bob Mosher and I drew up the two other elevations, naturally in Mr. Wright's style. When they came back, Mr. Wright continued describing the house, using the added elevations to reinforce his presentation. Second thoughts? The basic design never changed—pure all the way.

Architect's Sketch
of House.

Mr. Kaufmann soon left, drawing continued, and a few days later Mr. Wright went to Pittsburgh, this time carrying still more drawings under his arm, including perspectives marvelously done with colored pencils. More color upon color, day after day—lastly, lavender for haze.

While he was designing, he kept up a running monologue, always with the client in mind. "The rock on which E.J. sits will be the hearth, coming right out of the floor, the fire burning just behind it. The warming kettle will fit into the wall here. It will swing into the fire, boiling the water. Steam will permeate the atmosphere. You'll hear the hiss . . ." His pencil broke. One of us handed him another.

And always so sure of materials. "The vertical stone walls will be on solid rock, the horizontal slabs of poured concrete, set in like concrete shelves." Then he visualized the approach. "You arrive at the rear, with the rock cliff on your right and the entrance door to the left. Concrete trellises above. Rhododendra and big old trees everywhere—save the trees, design around them. The sound of the waterfall as background." Design for people.

Fireplace for Fallingwater during construction; concave circular form receives kettle.

Top: Mr. Wright called the concrete forms "bolsters"—
construction up to first floor.

Bottom: Contractor's shanty on second-floor balcony of
Fallingwater, placed in our absence in exactly the wrong
location.

Entrance road to Fallingwater, rock ledge at left.

Winter, 1935: The second Fellowship trek to Arizona, where we produced the working drawings and also those for the Hanna "Honeycomb House" in Stanford. Both houses would eventually be given to the public by their owners.

Spring, 1936: Bob Mosher went to Fallingwater to start supervision from the bottom up. I took it later from the second level to the top. Meanwhile, we were working on the Johnson Building for Racine, other new commissions . . . Mr. Wright was again a busy architect after a dozen years of doldrums and disregard. The Fellowship was to be his springboard back to creativity. We apprentices were young. Inexperienced. Willing. Devoted. He taught us his way, we couldn't miss, there was an awakening in architecture, and we were in its midst.

Paul R. Hanna "Honeycomb House," Stanford, California, 1937.

9

At nineteen, studying architecture at New York University, I found in the school library a volume of Frank Lloyd Wright's *Princeton Lectures.* I'd already read everything I could find by and about him—I was captivated by his designs. But here he seemed to be speaking out of the pages directly to me.

He was saying to the young man, start anew, keeping your inspirations, look to a new orderly way . . . human and scientific horizons, keep dignity. Words such as dignity, the individual . . . and with these elements, and a sense of order you can become an architect. The word "architect" was grandeur.

He was writing about the need for law and for nature—always the word "nature"—do not fear law. You will be for law if you are for nature. He went on discussing principle, how it was needed to gain the ends of accomplishment.

I read a newspaper account of a proposed Wright school. That did it. Not yet twenty, living in the depths of the Depression, I made up my mind to leave everything I'd known till then and go off to join Frank Lloyd Wright's grand scheme—the Taliesin Fellowship. There was a hero!

I thought to myself, "I'd better hurry. The man's already in his sixties . . . better get out there fast and learn what I can soon."

Going to Taliesin meant leaving family, friends, college, whatever material security there was in those days. But it didn't mean overturning my ideas and giving myself over to a whole new philosophy. No. Taliesin and Mr. Wright's ideas only seemed a natural outgrowth of the kind of thinking I'd grown up with.

My family was anything but establishment. My parents, who were born in Russia, had a penchant for social change and high cultural ideals. "Greatness" was much discussed in our apartment on New York's upper West Side, a neighborhood of business owners and executives. Both my father and mother were devotees of outstanding personalities. They were in the high fashion dress business—mother, the designer.

They tried hard to give us—my older brother and myself—an appreciation of the finest. As parents do, they soon extended their ideals and expectations to us. We boys were not only to admire greatness, we were to aspire toward greatness. Awareness of these demands and sensitivity to the very highest in human expression became a constant current throughout my young days, at home and at school.

In Mr. Wright, I found my own great man. I never discussed my feelings with him in exactly these terms, but he must have had an idea of my thoughts, knowing my background as he did. It's not that I chose only to study under Mr. Wright. Here was the giant to look up to, the creative source to draw from and give form and character and clarity to what, some day, might be my own ideas. I didn't think I could emulate such a giant, or anyone for that matter. I didn't believe my ideas were especially creative or original, unlike many young people who begin architecture convinced that their buildings will change the world. On the other hand, I was never one to copy or parrot what I found around. By twenty, my spirit was already independent, and the next nine years in the Taliesin Fellowship made me more so, more myself and not a flat, faded image of someone else's genius. This, I think, is the germ of my unique relationship with Mr. Wright—and possibly the cause of later difficulties.

Independence had always been given full license in my family. My schooling was more than progressive. It was quite extraordinary. When I was about eight, the family moved to New Jersey to join a colony. A group had organized as single-taxers, in the Henry George fashion, bought up land, put roads through, built houses, paid their "single tax" to the county as a farm. They set up their own school, where I was to go. The school was run on a simple system—learning by doing.

The educational process was something less than formal; the school demanded no discipline. A combination of arts and crafts, gardening and vegetable farming, and sports gave us vigorous spirits, but our academic training was a bit flimsy.

Nor was the teaching staff at all traditional. For example, "Uncle Scott" was the printing teacher, and since the children were taught to read by setting type and working the press, he had an important academic responsibility. Uncle Scott was a completely self-educated man. He'd grown up on a farm in Missouri, but he must have been quite literate, because when he wasn't teaching us, he worked as a proofreader for *The New York Times.* Uncle Scott was also the champion marble player, and in marble season he was with us outside, by the road that ran past the school, shooting his glass "immies." We admired a player so powerful that he could take an "aggie" and hit an immie and break it at great distance. In the printshop, we worked the presses and memorized all the cases for the letters. We learned to set type backwards, so it would give the correct image when printed. The most difficult thing was trying to keep our fingers out of the press. For us, the printshop wasn't just a game. We actually printed all the stationery for the school and our own school magazine, as well as separate articles written by the adults in the community.

When our Ferrer School, named after a martyred Spanish freethinker, first set up, some innovative people incorporated the concepts of Froebel into the primary-level curriculum. By now, Froebel's kindergarten has become so much a part of education that we don't even think of it, but in the mid-nineteenth century, when he worked out his idea for preschool education, the concept was revolutionary. He gave much thought to channeling play-energy into constructive learning patterns and into a child's spontaneity. The toys he designed, known as "gifts," consisted mainly of beautiful, smooth, natural wood blocks in simple geometric shapes.

The cube, cylinder, and sphere were the first toys given to the young child, and each set of gifts was progressively more challenging. Along with the basic wood blocks, there were other structured teaching gifts, such as colored paper for plaiting, cardboard shapes to fit together, paper for folding into three-dimensional forms, and beads and string for hanging objects.

For the more sophisticated students in our school, there were entire workshops—adjacent to the printshop—for weaving and ceramics. We built a separate workshop near by for carpentry. At perhaps eleven or twelve, I corralled a couple of kids into building a whole model-sized village. We designed it outdoors, near the main school building, at the confluence of the brook and the larger stream where we all used to swim naked—adults, children, everybody. It was a natural spot for our village and well protected. We children constructed roads and houses and a school. In the carpentry shop, I made automobiles and trucks to scale in wood, with tiny axles and springs so they'd bounce along as we played with them.

My folks were always organizing some event for the community. Often they'd arrange a benefit concert program and bring out a dancer, a pianist, a singer for a Saturday night's entertainment at the school. They cajoled their customers, the young and aspiring ones, into performing for our school, for fund raising.

At one period, because my parents were commuting to their business in New York every day and couldn't be around to look after me, I lived in the school's dormitory. Many people in the colony were in the garment business and, like my parents, also commuted, so we were a large group together in the dorms. There was a boy's dorm down at one end, a big common living room, then the girl's dorm. The buildings had been part of a farm, and the old barn was our favorite play place. The kitchen and dining hall were located in the old farmhouse; the director of the school and his wife lived upstairs.

In our daily studies we were never introduced to formal academic subjects. No history, no social studies or anything of that sort. We learned geography by saving foreign stamps and by identifying their origins, and in no time we knew the size and location of nearly every country in the world. I used to make pilgrimages into New York to the city's stamp shops to enlarge my collection. We all wrote away to stamp dealers around the country for "approvals."

We all did reading on our own. Somehow, we did get some math, probably through the necessities of carpentry. From time to time there would be a parents' revolt—the adults would become concerned that their children weren't learning how to read or count properly. Then the school would institute some regular classes in these subjects—to keep the parents calm. But the classes never lasted for long.

In the summers, too, we were busy "learning." One of the teachers, Uncle Ferm (all the teachers were called "Uncle"), had some land in northern New Jersey, about sixty miles away. We'd hike up there, taking a couple of days for the trek, and camp out for two or three weeks in tents, cooking our own meals and washing in a cold, cold stream. It's curious that even though I spent much time outdoors, had my own garden, learned to prune trees and grow things, I was never consumed by a passion for nature. I wasn't much of a romantic.

Some years later, in one of their periodic financial depressions, my folks changed their mind about colony life and we moved back to Manhattan. My father now had a wholesale dress business; mother was still the designer. She designed dresses for actresses, opera singers, and vaudevillians. When I was very small, I was playing in the shop when a prima donna came in for a fitting. My mother put me up on the star's knee and said, "Madame Galli-Curci, sing a song for my boy!" I couldn't have been more than five, but such memories are still clear.

Many years later, Mr. Wright was in town and he came into their shop to pick out a dress for Mrs. Wright. "Mother Tafel," he asked, "how do you go about designing a dress?" "Why, Mr. Wright," she answered, "the same way you go about designing a building! I lift up the fabric, see how it falls and drapes, get an idea, make a cut with the scissors, and I'm off. A dress to make a woman beautiful."

Settled again in New York, my parents began to worry that I'd never have any "real education." After all, my earlier schooling was like a long stretch of summer camp, for years on end. They sent me first to a private high school, but my interests were scarcely academic. At the colony school, I'd never really learned the discipline of study, so the jump to a private school in the city was difficult. The art classes and carpentry and theater held all my attention. Eventually, I took evening classes at the neighborhood high school to get a college entrance diploma.

Probably under my parents' influence, I developed a great enthusiasm for the theater and joined a puppet group in the Village. The company did frequent shows, and even produced an adaptation of Eugene O'Neill's *Hairy Ape,* which we put on at the New School.

One summer I worked backstage in a theater at an adult camp in the Adirondacks, constructing and changing sets, pulling the curtain, operating lights. During the winters my brother and I went regularly to concerts, operas, and theater performances where family customers appeared, from Broadway to the fringes of New York. One season while I was still in high school, I was a stand-in usher every other Thursday in the second balcony at

While bidding me farewell before I went home for a holiday visit, Mr. Wright went into the vault and returned with a Japanese print, saying, "Give this to your mother." The inscription on the upper left-hand corner reads: "To Mother Tafel, Xmas '38 FLLW."

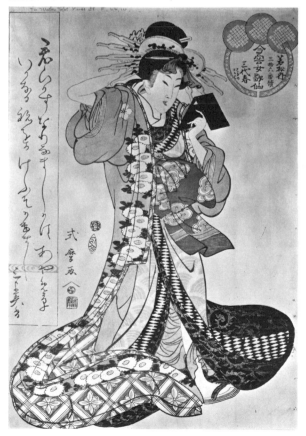

Carnegie Hall. For this, you didn't even have to know where the seats were—it was a concert series and subscribers knew where they belonged. I was devoted to the piano and progressed as far as the Brahms intermezzi and the Beethoven sonatas. I wasn't wild, but I was active, chasing girls and going to parties.

One day, in the middle of a piano lesson, when I obviously wasn't putting much effort into the music, my teacher stopped me and asked, "Edgar, what do you want to be for the rest of your life?" "An architect," I replied.

"Then why are you here studying the piano? Do what it takes to become an architect."

That started me off. Something inside my head suddenly shifted, turned, and went to work. Architecture! I understood then where I was headed, and my years of art and freedom no longer seemed an easy life, but background for a serious discipline.

A draftsman friend noted once that my thinking must already have been flowing on architectural lines. He pointed out that my skill in carpentry helped me visualize three-dimensionally and gave me a feeling for working with natural materials.

In my last year of high school, I read Lewis Mumford's *Sticks and Stones,* in which he described the new world of architecture. And I happened upon Louis Sullivan's *Autobiography of an Idea,* written in 1923 as that great innovator in American architecture looked back on his life. I wonder if I realized then what a monumental impression these books and Sullivan's personality made on me. To read Sullivan's joyful, exuberant, overflowing account of his childhood and young years—it was like looking into a mirror. I saw not only my own experiences, reflections of the family spirit, but also my own feelings—the delight in learning and making things with my own hands, the sense of order in nature, the wonder at the magnificent constructions of humans, the force of the trained mind, the fascination with the governing and all-powerful IDEA.

I wanted to go away to school, but the effects of the Depression wouldn't allow it. My folks offered instead to feed and clothe me and pay my tuition at a local college if I lived at home. There wasn't much of a choice—Columbia, with two years of pre-architectural study and four years of formal architecture, or New York University, with a full five-year program. NYU demanded a year less. It was cheaper. I was in a hurry. Therefore, NYU it was.

Architectural studies at NYU—on the thirteenth floor of an office building at Forty-third Street and Second Avenue—were far from dull. In the first year I went through history of architecture, freehand drawing and perspective, descriptive geometry, and some necessary liberal arts classes. As a result of my own temperament and my rather irregular earlier education, I didn't do well. I had absolutely no competitive spirit, didn't care about grades, and spent time only on the subjects that interested me. Those I took very seriously. To try to get through these studies faster, I planned to take courses during three summers and make up a full semester. That first summer of college, I went out to New Jersey to stay at my aunt's house and take some electives at Rutgers. The most successful was a course in drama, and I must have read a play a day for six weeks.

It was during that summer that I read Wright's *Autobiography*. I'd already stumbled onto other writings of his in the libraries—and the spark was lit. The first chapters of the *Autobiography* echoed my entire childhood. As I was graphically oriented, it was his designs that impressed me most, but I also felt right at home with his philosophy. There were no constraints in that thinking.

That year, too, was the memorable opening exhibit of the International School at the Museum of Modern Art. They tried to fit Wright into the group. Only one of his houses was exhibited—the House on the Mesa, which seemed pristine and certainly not in his usual style. Still, the show was exciting and Wright's house stood out even if he wasn't in compatible company.

In the first-year classes at college, we were allowed to show some influence of Wright in our design—such as it was. But after that, in the second year, we were supposed to turn to the "French modern" for influence and to the sand-papered Beaux-Arts style. Most of the educated and architecturally aware people I met and talked with about Wright knew *of* him, but only as a distant Midwesterner. There was nothing of his in New York that one could go to see.

One morning that summer—1932—my aunt handed me a clipping from the *Herald Tribune* announcing that Frank Lloyd Wright was starting his own school of architecture. I must have talked enough about him, and the impression he made on me, to prompt her to cut out that notice. I sent for the brochure on the Taliesin Fellowship. My courses at Rutgers ended in July. In August there was a job at a summer camp, working with puppets. The bulletin arrived after that.

It was printed in dark red ink on sepia paper and spelled out his glorious plan for fostering an authentic American culture, a grand program calling for seventy apprentices and seven master teacher-architects. I was captivated.

Back in New York, right after Labor Day, there were days and days of confusion. Should I drop everything and go study with Wright? Should I wait for the school to be fully organized and accepted? Should I continue at NYU? Suppose I did decide to go? Would he take me?

Seeking advice and prodded by my family, I went around to ask the few architects I knew for their opinions. I stopped by one noontime to see an old architect who worked in a diminished

office at a big rolltop desk. He took a sandwich out of his desk and ate as we talked, advising me to wait until Wright had time to get things going properly. Well, maybe he was right.

Many of the "art architects," as we called them, had studios in town where students and other young architects would come to work *en charrette* to get projects finished in time for competition deadlines. I went to question some of these fellows and dropped in on the Atelier Goodman. Young Percival Goodman said, "If I were you, I'd go." He encouraged me. "I wouldn't ask anyone's advice," he said. Well, maybe he was right.

My parents thought whatever I wanted was fine. No problem with them. I had an uncle, Uncle Arthur, an attorney. He had married into the family and was its only college graduate. Whatever Uncle Arthur suggested—in any situation—we knew that the opposite should be done. So when he said, with considerable vehemence, that I shouldn't go to Taliesin—that settled it. I was going.

My parents could afford the NYU tuition, $450. The Taliesin bulletin specified tuition of $675. Carefully, I filled out the forms and wrote to Mr. Wright, saying I wanted to join the Fellowship as an apprentice but that I only had $450.

I dropped the letter in the mailbox and waited. Weeks passed. Actually, only a long two weeks. New York's pavements gritted under me, and I wanted to exchange the city's concrete for Wisconsin's green. The telegram arrived, my first telegram:

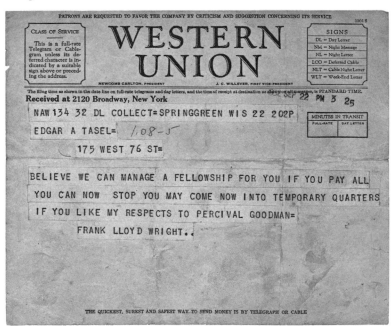

Going to join the Taliesin Fellowship! The certainty of it was a fever running through me, tingling to my fingertips. Suddenly everything around me turned secondary, transparent, empty. Mr. Wright's offer was very generous. After all, we were in the middle of the Depression and there wasn't much money for anything. He was always to be gracious about personal things; he could always compromise when necessary.

The days of preparation scarcely seemed real. It wasn't like going away to college. I was going off to a way of life. "What will happen?" I kept saying to myself. "Maybe I'll come back next year—but maybe I'll never come back. Who will I become?"

How was I to get out to Wisconsin? It was a very foreign part of the world. I was a New Yorker and it seemed to me that anything west of the Hudson River was the hinterland. How should I travel—by bus, by train? Finally I bought a one-way bus ticket to Chicago. What a feeling! The day I left, at the bus station, my mother took me aside and gave me a bottle of wine, warning, "Don't tell your father!" My father, in turn, made his farewell and slipped me a bottle of Canadian Club, whispering, "Don't tell your mother! And don't drink cheap whiskey!" It was still Prohibition. The whole way out to Chicago, I rode sitting next to a recent divorcée; we drank my mother's wine.

In Chicago, I changed buses for Madison, the nearest city to Spring Green. Spring Green was the town closest to Taliesin. How strange the Midwest looked. I was struck by completely different brand names for familiar products and later by the flat regional accent. I was fascinated. New country for a new life.

In Madison, I stopped for a day to catch my breath, stretch, and visit a friend at the university. As he showed me around the campus, I told him of my plans and expectations. I could feel the excitement bursting through my words. I couldn't unwind. Next morning I took the local bus to Spring Green, forty miles away. I don't suppose my excitement left me the common sense to telephone ahead to announce an arrival time. I should have written some time before, saying approximately when I'd be leaving New York. But no. I just appeared.

Spring Green. Small town in the heart of Middle America, no more than a railroad stop, a lumber yard, a feed mill. The population in 1932 couldn't have been more than 400, and the region was dotted with prosperous farms. At the edge of town was an abattoir; then came a couple of drygoods stores, a Ford garage, and a welding shop where farmers still brought their horses to be shod. I looked for the heavy, square State Bank designed by Wright in 1914—I'd seen the design in books. Later I learned that it had never been built.

A closer look at the town made me aware that there were two of everything—two bars, two dry goods stores, two banks, two funeral parlors. Later I found out that the town was part Catholic, part Protestant. All the businesses were divided rather uneconomically. Well, except for the lumber business. There wasn't enough of that to go around. The yard was run by Miss M. Cavanaugh; her name was printed on the doors of her truck and she was known as "Lady Logger." Oak railroad ties were her specialty. For entertainment, Spring Green offered one movie house, which also presented occasional vaudeville shows. The two town bars served beer and real but very raw whiskey, locally produced and mellowed twenty-four hours. In the middle of town was a little bandstand. On Wednesday nights in the summer, the high school band gave concerts while the stores stayed open late. Appreciation of the music was expressed by horn honking from the farmers in parked cars.

From the bus window, I'd had my tour of Spring Green. We stopped outside the one hotel, and our luggage was thrown down from the rack on the roof. With a New Yorker's aplomb, I went into the hotel and asked how to get to "Wright's." The lady at the desk pointed to a roadster across the street and said, "Those people, the Fritzes, belong out there. They'll take you

over." I walked to the car and introduced myself, saying I was a new apprentice at Taliesin. Herbert Fritz had worked for Wright, an apprentice in the old style. He'd come up from Chicago as a draftsman, fallen in love with a mason's daughter, married her, and raised a family. Later both his son and daughter became Taliesin apprentices. Herb explained that Mr. Wright was over at Hillside, the complex of buildings near Taliesin that had been a school run by Wright's aunts. I climbed into the rumble seat and we drove off directly, out of Spring Green through the river valley and rolling countryside, very beautiful with its strange, rough outcroppings of stone. Herb dropped me with all my luggage at the door of what had been the Hillside School gym and was becoming the theater, work in progress.

In spite of travel weariness and my attempts at outer calm, I

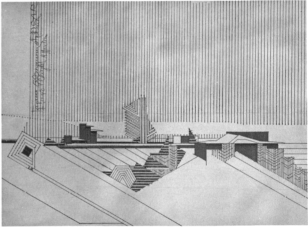

Christmas card designed by artist-apprentice Eugene Masselink. The inscription reads: "EDGAR Taliesin Olgivanna Frank Lloyd Wright Affection." Mr. Wright enjoyed inscribing. *Left:* Same profile of Taliesin and the river valley.

felt tight and held my breath as I stood in the doorway. "You've made it," I whispered to myself. At the far end of the room, on a raised platform serving as a stage, stood Mr. Wright. It was like coming into a presence. And what presence he had! He shot out electricity in every direction.

Near him were a grand piano and an old wind-up phonograph screeching out a Beethoven symphony. He was testing the acoustics. I crossed the room, still holding my breath, and said, "Mr. Wright, I'm Edgar Tafel. From New York."

He had a special way of shaking hands, simply raising his arm bent at the elbow and holding his hand there to be grasped, drawing people to him. "Young man," he addressed me, "help move this piano."

He adored moving pianos around, it turned out. When he entered a room, the piano—if there was one—was the first thing he rearranged. Wherever he went, he insisted on moving furniture—he always rearranged flowers in their vases.

There were others in the room: a theater-seat salesman and his wife. All of us were driven, by an apprentice, from Hillside around the hill to Taliesin.

At Taliesin we went through a Dutch door, its top half swinging open. Below, flagstone, and all around us natural stone. The ceiling was low, sandy plaster just above our heads. Mr. Wright led the way into his living room. What an impression that room made! It was my first total Frank Lloyd Wright atmosphere. How I was struck by those forms, shapes, materials! It was breathtaking—I had never imagined such beauty and harmony.

A little way into the room, the ceiling rose from a light deck—the space opened up. From the entrance, as I stood near a cabinet about five feet high, my eyes skimmed over an Oriental figure and went right to the two bands of window on the opposite walls. Way to the left I saw the fireplace, with its great stone hearth, and a Steinway grand. The bands of windows framed a view across a valley.

Mrs. Wright came in and Mr. Wright introduced me to this impressively regal woman. "Mother," he said, for he often used this endearment, "this is Edgar Tafel. From New York." He had the rare gift of kings and statesmen, that of remembering names and identifying characteristics of the people he met. Mrs. Wright graciously welcomed me to Taliesin.

Mr. Wright was quite short, a surprise. He had described himself in the *Autobiography* as five feet eight-and-a-half inches, but still I was expecting a giant, or a man at least six feet tall. Perhaps because he wasn't tall, he also seemed stockier than I had expected. I remember very clearly that, when I first saw him, he wore a pair of tweed trousers fastened tightly at the ankle with matching cloth ties. The style seemed peculiar, but it was for protection against the weather, so the cold couldn't get up his

Taliesin living room, bands of glass, cast-iron figure.

Top: Living room, toward dining area—balcony above, at right.

Bottom left: View into valley.

Bottom right: "Staccato" clerestory windows cast varied changing sunlight into center of space.

Taliesin drafting room. Stairs at left lead to balcony
(with grand piano) over vault. In this studio,
Mr. Wright designed hundreds of buildings.

trouser legs and also so that the pants wouldn't flap around. In
public, he generally wore a trim porkpie hat, which he sometimes
abandoned for a soft beret. A tailor in Chicago, Stevenson on
Michigan Avenue, made up the clothing Mr. Wright designed
for himself. He never dressed outlandishly, but he certainly had
a definite style. There were his capes, which made him appear
seven feet tall when he swirled them over his shoulder, and he
always wore stiff, high-starched detachable shirt collars. When
he was in Japan, working on the Imperial Hotel, he ordered some
new collars from a local haberdasher. He explained how he
wanted them made, and a sample was sent for his approval. He
scribbled in red: "OK, FLLW." When the collars were delivered, every one was monogrammed "OK, FLLW" in red ink.

He loved to wear a flower in his lapel. On entering a
restaurant, he'd grab a flower from the nearest table and stick it in
his lapel.

Mr. Wright never just walked. He strutted. He marched. He strode. He entered a room like a king entering his audience chamber, Mrs. Wright behind him like a queen. Perhaps that special upbeat in his walk came from wearing shoes with an elevated heel. Even when he got older, he walked with grace and a certain lilt. Usually, too, he carried a cane, but that was a mere stage prop, a mace, used for effect. All his movements showed a natural, animal grace.

As long as I knew him, Mr. Wright suffered from a stiff neck. Since he couldn't turn his head easily, he twisted his entire upper torso when he had to look around. Oddly, even this gesture never seemed awkward. He moved so fluidly that his smallest gesture had elegance.

Mr. Wright's accent was pure Midwest. The voice had great strength, coming from deep in the chest. He rarely talked in a whisper. How could he? He was always claiming, declaiming, pontificating. He loved to bellow out a tired phrase: "America is the only country to have gone from a state of barbarism to a state of decadence with no intervening culture." The simplest statement, from his tongue, became a graven, immutable truth for all ages, even if it was just about the weather.

Everything about Mr. Wright's stature and presence showed that he clearly thought of himself as a living legend and loved acting out the role. And each new day was for new enjoyment.

During my nine years with the Taliesin Fellowship and after that, in all the years I knew Mr. Wright, I felt we had a special relationship. Maybe he instilled this feeling in most people who knew him well. By the time I got to Taliesin, I had a well-developed sense of fun. Mr. Wright soon came to think of me as a "Peck's Bad Boy" type, and I think he had an affection for me because of that independence. In those first years of the Fellowship, I was a solid member of the small core who became truly serious about his architecture. We felt we were the heart of the Fellowship, the reason for its existence. Maybe it was to us that Mr. Wright looked to help fulfill his dream. The total devotion each of us felt toward him was expressed in different ways, tinted by our different personalities. Many apprentices were afraid of "Daddy Frank," as Mrs. Wright's daughter, his stepdaughter Svetlana, called him. We used to call him Daddy Frank too, behind his back. Somehow my respect and love for the man were never colored by fear of his authority and greatness. In fact, I even dared to tell him slightly risqué stories, which seemed to amuse him.

Later, I would make little business trips for him or take care of special things around Taliesin. Once we were driving back to Wisconsin after a winter at Taliesin West in Arizona and there

Top: Posing for a picture at a picnic.
Bottom: Jesting in carriage before going to a picnic.

was trouble with the car in Colorado. It was brand new, but it broke down. I thought the repair should be the manufacturer's responsibility, so I took it upon myself to write a letter of complaint to the Ford Motor Company dealer, who sent us a check by return mail. Another time, I put an ad in the local Spring Green newspaper for a farmer and a gardener and interviewed all the applicants. When I was working in Racine on the Johnson Wax Building, Mr. Wright—who was busy with apprentices in Arizona at the end of winter—asked me to help get Taliesin ready for the Fellowship's return. He relied on me to take care of special details in the everyday operation of the Fellowship. That responsibility was helpful in preparing me to handle the business of my own practice later.

During my years in the Fellowship, and I suppose in all the years until Mr. Wright's death—and probably even after his death—it was inevitable that many apprentices resented Mr. Wright and formed a bloc of disagreement concerning his personality and the way he ran Taliesin. Many who gave him lip service seemed not really to appreciate the quality of his genius. For the most part, these were the people outside the drafting room—the marginal folk who spent all their time in the garden, in the kitchen, or at their hobbies, people who came to Taliesin not so much to produce architecture under Mr. Wright as to take part in a way of life that was appealing for many reasons. Because these people were less interested in architecture, they may have been less exposed to the beauty of Mr. Wright's genius.

My attitude was that if you could be useful to him, and if you could make yourself a part of his way of living and thinking, instead of fighting it, you could gain a great deal for yourself. As an earnest apprentice, you were an extension of Mr. Wright. Mr. Wright had so served Sullivan—a pencil in the hand of the master. That may be the best way to be yourself. It worked for me.

None of the apprentices expected to be geniuses—just good, solid creative people. But we always had a few apprentices at Taliesin who came out and wanted to design factories or high-rise buildings immediately. They didn't understand the idea of service, of slowly absorbing, working, learning by doing and watching and following the master.

The trouble in this situation, in having this attitude of reverence toward Mr. Wright, is that many people outside Taliesin, especially critics and writers, mistook our devotion for subservience. Mr. Wright didn't want subservience.

He wanted devotion to the cause of an organic architecture—integration of form, materials indigenous to the setting, and function. And there is a difference between the servant and the devoted apprentice. Perhaps, in order to run Taliesin effectively, he needed all levels of devotion.

Here is the fundamental problem, and it's not simply a

problem with Mr. Wright and the relationship of the Taliesin apprentices to him. It is the basic problem of dealing with genius—in any age, any discipline. How could we express ourselves as individuals if we were only extensions of Mr. Wright? How could we feel and express our complete devotion without being slavish? And how could we develop and feel free to express our own individualities without abandoning Mr. Wright's philosophy and the cause of organic architecture? In a way we could, and in a way we couldn't.

In the drafting room, all we could do was execute the drawings the way we thought Mr. Wright wanted them. During the years of the learning period, we often spent our free time in our rooms drawing anything we wanted, designing projects from imagination. Years later, when the Fellowship progressed to the point where several of us started to bring in jobs on our own, we did the actual designing ourselves. Of course, we wanted Mr. Wright's approval and suggestions, and he was always generous about helping us. We didn't feel then that we were designing in a derivative style. We'd been trained at Taliesin, and our training became our thinking. Our designs were our own, even if they came from a recognizable style.

After I'd left Taliesin, worked for a while in offices, then spent two years in India during the war, I came back to start a practice of my own. Immediately I was bothered by an enormous problem of identity.

If I emphasized my long association with Mr. Wright and still declared a formal attachment to Taliesin, I'd be branded by the establishment as "just another Wright disciple." Yet I certainly didn't want to dissociate myself from Mr. Wright, either in philosophy or in any working relationship. I'd seen other Taliesin apprentices develop in one of two ways: Either they clung to Taliesin permanently as their adoptive home and spiritual stronghold or they turned away and became completely independent, choosing divergent architectural paths. Very, very few of Mr. Wright's students continued the relationship while still retaining their own identity in architecture.

Mr. Wright inspecting Broadacre City model, suggesting additions and refinements.

2

rank Lloyd Wright died in 1959, at the age of 91. His image was familiar around the world. Those of you who saw him, heard him speak, read articles about him in his last years, pictured him as a grand old man with white hair, a cane, and a rebellious nature. He had looked much the same since the 1930s and was certainly well known beyond the architectural sphere for his seemingly cantankerous individualist spirit.

Mr. Wright was born in 1867, when America was less than half her present age and the first Centennial had not yet been marked. The Civil War was barely over, the nation was facing Reconstruction. Hardly more than twenty years earlier, Texas had been an independent country, and in 1867 most of the areas west of the Mississippi hadn't even been admitted to the Union as states. The political scandals at every level and financial disasters of the 1870s were just on the horizon. For the moment, this was still frontier America, with plenty of virgin land to explore and all the room a man could want to expand his ideas and stretch his sense of individuality.

When Wright made his entrance as an architect—at birth that is, for his mother was determined to have a son and to make him a great architect—Walt Whitman was celebrating the Individual in poetry. *Leaves of Grass* had appeared in 1855. The essays of Emerson and Thoreau had a fresh, inspiring ring to the American spirit. The sweep of social reform in Europe eddied across the Atlantic, and America again became the refuge for groups of political, social, and religious idealists who set up their own new utopian communities—Amana, Oneida, the Roycrofters, and others. The scientific world had just been thrown into a revolution by Darwin's *On the Origin of Species* (1859).

A generation earlier, when Wright's parents were born, both Europe and America were deep in war. Having barely recovered from Napoleon, the continent erupted in revolutions. The days of the empires were fading fast, and nationalism was becoming the byword for everyone, from politicians to composers.

Wright's father, William Russell Cary Wright, was born in 1825 in New England of an English family with strong non-establishment religious views. His father had been a Baptist minister, and William Wright also became a preacher, though music held a greater place in his heart. One can see reflections of his strong temperament and powerful ego in his son Frank. It was from his father also that son Frank acquired a deep sensitivity to music, especially the geometric compositions of Bach. Throughout his adult life, William Wright vacillated between teaching music and preaching religion, never being very successful at either. He was even less successful at heading a family and bringing up children. Driven by a search for inner satisfaction, William Wright moved restlessly about the country, from New England to the Midwest. His first wife had died in 1864, and William Wright did not seem to have much concern for his three children by that marriage. When his wanderings took him in the vicinity of Spring Green, Wisconsin, he met and soon married a teacher, Anna Lloyd Jones, spirited member of a large clan.

The biographical accounts of Frank Lloyd Wright, as well as his own conversation, reveal clearly that his mother Anna had a far more stable and resolute character than the man she married. In fact, Mr. Wright was so extremely close to his mother that he often kept her with him at Taliesin. When he was in Japan working on the Imperial Hotel, his mother—who was not especially strong at the age of eighty—insisted on sailing across the Pacific to take care of him upon hearing he was ill. From the Fellowship years, I remember a three-foot square painted portrait of her that was placed prominently in the Taliesin drafting room, over the fireplace. Mr. Wright rarely spoke of his mother, or indeed of any family member, but I have heard that she had quite a sense of humor, in addition to her intelligence and firmness. Antonin Raymond, the architect who worked for a while with Mr. Wright on the Imperial Hotel, said that Anna Wright, while visiting in Japan, often substituted the names of famous Japanese artists for everyday people and things. She'd say, "Please call Hokusai and tell him to hurry up with my breakfast. I'm dying to go for a ride in my Hiroshige." I once saw a letter in the files from Mr. Wright to his mother. As I recollect, it said: "Dear

Hillside complex from the air, September 1930.

Mother—I haven't written you for so long because I've been busy with work. You know, if you hadn't given me such a big nose, I wouldn't be obligated to keep it so close to the grindstone."

Anna Lloyd Jones' strong-minded, strong-willed, Bible-loving Unitarian clan left Wales for the American Midwest in 1845 and found a country to their liking in Wisconsin. They took over the land, built their farms, and developed great pride and love for their new home. The Lloyd Joneses were not merely successful farmers. With their intense respect for education and devotion to a Christian life stripped of excess, the family produced ministers and educators and was actively involved in the social reforms of the day. Uncle Jenkin Lloyd Jones looked after his sizable congregation in Chicago's All Souls' Church and worked with Jane Addams and others in trying to create a model life for modern America. Mr. Wright's two maiden aunts, Nell and Jane, turned their sprightly energies to young people, directing the Hillside Home School—near Spring Green—in the 1890s. They asked Wright to design a number of school buildings at the turn of the century. The school's approach to education, radical for its time, received much attention. Its coeducational enrollment policy and practical work programs were unusual in a world of Victorian thinking.

Throughout her son Frank's childhood, Anna Lloyd Jones

Hillside. Left to right: terrace, rebuilt theater, kitchen and dining room. "Romeo and Juliet" windmill barely shows in the background.

Top left: Rebuilding former architect Silsbee's Hillside building. Mr. Wright later had it torn down.

Middle left: Dilapidated condition in 1932.

Bottom left: Rebuilt by Mr. Wright and the Fellowship.

Below: Windmill, resurfaced with cypress board and batten siding, again pumps water.

Wright devoted her talents to his education. No one seems to have fathomed why she so fervently wanted him to become an architect. All biographical accounts, and his own picturesque narrative in the *Autobiography,* describe the engravings with which Mother Wright decorated the room where her son's crib was to stand. She chose English cathedrals, reproductions of ten wood-engravings—framed in oak. Direct and practical as she may have been, Anna Wright believed in mysterious, prenatal influences on her boy.

While the Wrights were visiting the Centennial Exposition held in Philadelphia in 1876, Mrs. Wright made a discovery that would leave a deep trace on her son's architectural career: Froebel. An exhibit at the fair demonstrated Froebel's ideas of a kindergarten, revolutionary for that day, and displayed his instructive "gifts"—many-shaped wooden blocks.

William Wright led his family to Massachusetts, where he was minister of a Baptist church in Weymouth for a few years, then back to the Midwest, to Madison, where he tried to organize a private music school in addition to his church work and public-speaking engagements. In 1885, after increasing discord, William Wright left his family, obtained a divorce, and never returned. Soon after, Frank, who was about sixteen, left high school and went to work to increase the family's income. To further her dream, Anna Wright arranged for her son to work as a bottom-level apprentice and general office helper for a professor of engineering.

While his mother's designs for his future in architecture were being nurtured, there was another, equally dynamic influence at work on the sensitivities of young Frank Wright: the magnificence, power, organization, beauty, and friendliness of nature—experienced in summers spent working on Uncle James Lloyd Jones' farm near Spring Green. His own description of farm life—the rigorous routine and constant fatigue, "adding tired to tired," the home-grown food and tremendous home-cooked meals, milking the cows and feeding the calves, putting up fences, weekly baths, Sunday picnics with the whole clan—all these experiences all jump brightly to life in the *Autobiography.* In addition to the exhilaration of honest outdoor work, the boy was learning to sense the deep mysteries of nature.

While working for the professor, Wright began courses as a part-time student at the University of Wisconsin. His studies lasted only a few semesters. He gave his formal architectural and engineering studies so little time and attention that they had practically no effect upon him. Concerning architecture, Wright was as naïve as the prairie. On the other hand, during the two years that he worked in the engineer's office, he learned mechanical drafting and saw the daily applications of practical engineering. By the time he was nineteen, Wright had an idea of who he was and what he wanted.

He found work with Chicago architect Silsbee, who had designed the buildings at the Hillside School and the family chapel near by, and then with Adler and Sullivan, the apex of the Chicago School. Sullivan took the young man under his wing and gave him great design responsibility, while Adler, the engineer, saw that the designs got built. This combination ground into one man all the requirements to become the total architect—sensitivity to form, function, materials, and construction.

Throughout his life, Mr. Wright felt that America had never been given—or had never taken—the chance to develop an indigenous, authentic architecture. For him, European culture was always the wolf at the edge of the yard, ready to devour whatever American culture was managing to germinate. He considered his chief mission in architecture and in life to hold the enemy at bay, to create and help sustain a genuinely American architecture and style of living, wholly personal and original. This was the driving idea behind the Prairie School movement, of which Mr. Wright was the leading figure in the first decade of this century, and again, though for a different set of reasons, of the Taliesin Fellowship beginning in the 1930s.

No matter what sociological, historical, or architectural views one holds, there are currents in the growth of American culture that can be recognized, though different schools of thought explain them in different ways.

In the last part of the nineteenth century, American thinking was divided into two mainstreams—the Midwest frontier and the Eastern establishment. The East may not have been old, speaking historically, but it certainly was traditional, with its Founding Fathers, thirteen original colonies, Liberty Bell, and Pilgrims. All from Europe. Architecture in the nation reflected that spirit. America looked backward, to Europe, for her architecture.

The young man who wanted to study architecture went—after a few years of college in America—to France to study at the Ecole des Beaux-Arts, the highest and most impressive peak of status-appeal architectural education. A stay in France had to be accompanied by the grand tour across Europe, from Big Ben to the Sistine Chapel. Italy, especially, meant months in the sun, absorbing Mediterranean habits, languishing with a sketchbook in front of cathedrals, passing plenty of time in the artists' cafés. Then the student, having become a real gentleman, would return to New York or Boston or Philadelphia with a collection of sketches and books.

But how did he design? He looked at his books, took a column order from one architectural masterpiece, a window detail from another, an arch from here, a pilaster from there, and that was architecture. In a not too general way, that does describe nineteenth-century architecture. The young American who went abroad to polish his education simply brought back the

Family Unitarian chapel and graveyard.

past century's tired and by now preposterous reworkings of earlier ages' masterpieces. It was time for something new. This was what we kept hearing all the time—at Taliesin.

Architects' clients in the Midwest at that time were very cautious; they sought the Respectable for their buildings. They also turned eastward, thinking to buy security among the older traditions. After all, the East was where the money was, as well as being the heart of transportation and communication with the rest of the "cultured" world. All the grand projects were financed in the East—railroads, large-scale building schemes, and the rest. The gold system, on which financing was based, was the enemy of the westerner.

The Midwest? That was all new. There was Chicago, and beyond, the Great Plains. To Louis Sullivan, arriving in Chicago as a young architect about 1873, it had seemed wild, crude, exciting—having all the elements of a frontier. He had vision.

Something happened in Chicago about 1880, an extraordinary kind of phenomenon that flourished for perhaps two decades and then faded away, snuffed out by the wholesale acceptance of Eastern culture. The phenomenon, actually a revolution, had two manifestations, one after the other, and together they constituted the beginnings of a true American architecture: the skyscraper and the Prairie house.

A variety of causes contributed to the genesis of what has become the typically American building, the high-rise office or factory or apartment building—the skyscraper. In October 1871, during two days and two nights, a great fire carried by high winds devastated Chicago. The city's heart was charred and fallen. Over 20,000 buildings were gone, among them Chicago's best. Money for rebuilding was tight, and in 1873, when the federal government "demonetized" silver, the nation was thrown into a financial panic. The building industry stopped dead. Chicago took the phoenix image to heart and fought her way back up out of the ashes, but it would take another ten years for finance, technology, and manpower to permit reconstruction. To build this new city, Chicago fortunately had some fine engineers, eager to experiment.

Until that time, most big buildings were masonry, brick or stone. The invention of the elevator and its development as a passenger car in the middle of the nineteenth century—plus such advances as fireproofing, electricity, and the self-supporting metal (structural) frame—led architects and engineers to consider taller and taller structures. The urban squeeze was already beginning to be felt, and buildings were forced upward rather than out. But if you're building in brick, by the time you get up sixteen stories, the height of the Monadnock Building, you've got walls six feet thick on the ground floor to support the weight of the building above. Clearly, this wasn't practical or economical.

Sullivan's building for Schlesinger and Meyer (now Carson, Pirie, Scott and Co.), Chicago, Illinois.
Left: "Souvenir" from elevators in same building. Mr. Wright referred to it as "decadent Sullivan."

In the 1880s and the 1890s, downtown Chicago's skyline took on a totally new, modern face. One after the other, tall buildings grew up—ten, twelve, fifteen, even twenty-three stories high, forming a unified cityscape. The buildings fitted honestly together and fitted into the environment around them. The Carson, Pirie, Scott Store, the Gage Building, the Tacoma Building, the Manhattan, the Reliance Building, the Marshall Field Warehouse, the Auditorium Building (theater and hotel together), these and other landmarks of the period were the architecture of what we now call the Chicago School. I first saw some of them forty years after they were put up, and they were still crisp, sure, strong.

It is easy enough to explain why the Chicago School produced chiefly commercial structures. The city was then an immensely busy and prosperous focal point in the flow of goods, services, humanity—yes, and culture—back and forth across the country. As the financial and economic tensions of the 1870s lessened, business in the Midwest mushroomed. Chicago needed office buildings. It needed factories, stores, warehouses, and soon apartment houses. Before construction was even finished, office buildings were fully rented and the new tenants were ready with all their equipment to take over their space. Good fortune or the coincidences of history supplied not only a fast-developing technology for visionary architects and engineers, but also adventurous businessmen as clients, men who were not afraid of experimenting with the new.

What characterized the tall buildings of the Chicago School—in addition to boldness and innovative courage—was the use of a metal skeleton frame as the organizing structural system coupled with realistic clarity of design. Use and purpose of each building were carefully considered in the design process. Every element in the building meant something. Gone was what Sullivan called "that insensate period of General-Grant-Gothic," gone were the layers of earlier nineteenth-century frill. In their place was an elegant array of bas-relief ornament arising from the nature of the building itself. The emphasis was on height, naturally, but these architects also had a particular concern for windows. In Chicago's narrow and sometimes dark streets, the new tall building had to provide as much natural light as possible, for development of the bare electric light bulb was in its early stages and electricity was expensive. Design considerations for ample light and air soon brought about the "Chicago window," a long band of horizontally accented windows. It's not hard to see, in these conceptions, the parent buildings of our familiar contemporary steel and glass towers, standing alone, glassed to excess.

The heroes of the Chicago School were unusual. Educated as architects, they also had a great interest in engineering and the new technology. Their concerns, moreover, were not restricted to their profession. The most celebrated of these architects were cultured men whose artistic tastes and abilities were highly developed. For the most part, their attitudes toward education were bravely antiestablishment. Although some of them had attended the fashionably proper institutions of formal learning, they realized all too clearly the disadvantages of a narrow and rigid academic point of view. Gathering knowledge and experience where they could, these were self-educated architects, unhindered by notions of "correctness" and "acceptability."

The names of these men are not as well known as they should be. William Le Baron Jenney, the grand old man of the group, was looked to for his brilliant engineering sense. There were three dynamic and successful partnerships: Burnham and Root, Holabird and Roche, Adler and Sullivan.

Louis H. Sullivan, more than any other individual, was the hope and promise of a complete American architecture. His was an impressive figure in the first era of tall buildings, and it was his ideas, not just his buildings, that overwhelmingly influenced the men around him and the younger generation of architects prominent after the turn of the century. Sullivan had vision. He had a profound understanding of the American state of mind and the appropriate nature of a new architecture.

The extraordinary new commercial architecture that took root in Chicago continued to be expressed in one sensible, straightforward, handsome building after another, not just in Chicago, but soon in other key cities, St. Louis and Buffalo. The force of this wholly fresh architectural thinking reasserted itself again and again, gaining impetus. Innovation and direct, sure-handed boldness ruled the day. Then, suddenly, courage and originality crashed to a halt. Chicago ran headlong into a failure of nerve. One single event marked the reversal: the Chicago fair of 1893.

The World's Columbian Exposition of 1893, celebrating the 400th anniversary of Columbus' discovery, was an entire world in itself, a microcosm representing all human thought, from commerce and industry to technology and all the arts, and revealing every level of human development along the way. On the canal-lined, beautifully landscaped site bordering Lake Michigan, vast areas were given over to the pavilions for machinery, electricity, mines, transportation, manufactures, the liberal arts, horticulture, forestry, and agriculture. From all over the world, crowds of visitors gathered. They crammed the exhibit halls and went away much impressed, even overwhelmed, by the splendors of the modern age. To Americans, the fair was a stupendous success.

European reactions, however, were skeptical, discerning in the tone of the exhibits a full-blown and rather naïve reproduction of past European culture. After all, the Paris exhibition of 1889, for which the Eiffel Tower was created, was still fresh in everyone's mind. Unconsciously or not, the Americans were uneasy that they might not be able to equal the French artistic powers. An insidious sense of cultural inferiority was beginning to take hold of the American spirit. And so, the Columbian fair, instead of promoting a vigorous American statement, merely presented a revived version of what Europe had already locked away in the drawers of its history.

Another factor, too, gave the Chicago fair a strange, disembodied quality. In many ways, the fair should have been held in New York and not at all in Chicago. In the years when the frontier mentality was still a vitalizing force in Chicago architecture, the big businessman of the East liked to think of his factory as a kind of vast palace. In mid-nineteenth century, he chose copies of Italian Renaissance facades—executed in cast iron—to represent his commercial grandeur. A walk today down New York's lower Broadway shows what these men had in mind. A hundred years later, their cast-iron architecture still speaks of classical grandeur. Eastern architectural firms by 1893 were skilled in carrying out these historical styles with great efficiency, for the practice, recognition, and study of architecture itself had by then become institutionalized.

It is precisely this architecture of the East, a watered-down European derivative, that came to Chicago to dominate the entire face of the fair. In the heartland of America, and in a time of extraordinarily rich and daring architectural effort, the world's fair turned to the French Beaux-Arts for style and inspiration. The directors of the fair—influenced by the East—imposed the classical mode. The result was not so much a pleasing uniformity of style in the fair buildings as the willful distortion of future American culture.

The total effect of this architecture was grand—but grand illusion. Columns, arches, and domes paraded around the reflecting basin, plaster architecture pretending to be marble. As theatrical scenery or a set of temporary buildings for a festival celebration, the White City was a success. The sad aftermath to the fair was that this disembalmed architecture became the model of American good taste.

Out of context and out of scale, classical-style buildings sprinkled across America were not only meaningless. They were laughable.

The Chicago architects sold out. Eastern classicism, borrowed from the academic rigidity of the Beaux-Arts, was jammed down their throats. They had to give in. Or so they felt.

At the fair, only one architect held out—Louis Sullivan. As the designer of the Transportation Building, with his partner Dankmar Adler, Sullivan was fortunate to have a site somewhat removed from the main axis (or maybe he was pushed aside). The Transportation Building, where trains and some of the first automobiles were to be displayed, was to stand on the edge of an irregular winding lagoon, which allowed an original architectural approach. With its bold entrance and detail reminiscent of temple sculpture in India, the Transportation Building proudly declared itself nontraditional. This is precisely the germ of the monumental disappointment both Sullivan and young Wright felt about the fair. Mr. Wright hoped that when the Europeans saw this new architecture of the Midwest—as he hoped again later, especially when his own work was published by Wasmuth, of Berlin, in 1910 they would open up. But no, he saw that they preferred to continue in their usual stick-together vein. It was to be just one more phase in squeeze-it-out-of-a-tube architecture that had been practiced since the Greeks. Yes, even the Greeks had their own ancient International style. Wherever they went, they reproduced Parthenons.

Frank Lloyd Wright, who had already been working for several years as a draftsman for Adler and Sullivan, never forgot Louis Sullivan's courage and strength of conviction in holding firm to his individuality as his colleagues succumbed to the attacks of incipient neoclassicism. With a broken heart, Sullivan says in his *Autobiography of an Idea,* written nearly thirty years after the

Entrance to Sullivan's Transportation Building, World's
Columbian Exposition, Chicago 1893.

fair, "The damage wrought by the World's Fair will last for half
a century from its date, if not longer." It lasted longer—much
longer.

We had to set up quarters for ourselves, and for the influx
of apprentices due to arrive during October 1932. Coming to
Taliesin shoved us at once into the reality of the world of building. My first job on the first day was to whitewash a couple of
bathrooms.

I guess we used whitewash, not paint, because it was
cheaper: lime and water. Some salt, maybe salt was the binder.
Then there were other rooms to fix up, beneath the family living
quarters and the studio, above the dining rooms. The half-dozen
of us who got there first got the best places and we banged them
together to suit ourselves—but in the Wright manner and under
his direction: low decks or ledges overhead, doors six feet and
two inches high, windows in odd shapes and places, built-in beds
and benches and tables. We changed them constantly, as we
found a board, a stone, some hardware.

The original group included a German architect, Henry

Apprentices Tafel and Yen Liang, having learned about masonry by constructing a pier, July 1933.

Klumb, who had had years with Mr. Wright. He led us, would eventually become a leading practitioner in Puerto Rico. John Howe, a recent high school graduate from the Prairie area, would become Mr. Wright's greatest "pencil in hand"; Wes Peters would become the Chief Architect of the Fellowship, giving his whole life to the cause. Yen Liang would eventually go back to China, return, and take his place as chief designer in a New York office . . . others would never become architects, would stay at the fringes.

Those who arrived in the ensuing weeks would take their respective places. Through the years, some stayed for short periods, some longer; the average stay, if there was an average, was two years. But during those first days, we oldsters were too busy to notice who was arriving.

My second day I got to help a real carpenter install partitions, toe-nailing the studs, cross-bracing, nailing up the wood lath. The lath came in bundles, rough slats forty-eight inches long, which were nailed horizontally across the two-by-four studs about a quarter-inch apart, so that the plaster would squeeze in between the lath and bind. The nails were special—black and galvanized, for the plaster lime burns everything. When I finished with the lath, I helped a laborer make a mound of mixed-up sand and lime with a hole in the middle for water. We puddled it into the shape of a doughnut. The result was called mud. When the plasterer called for "mud," I lugged it to him and helped slather it onto the lath. While the first coat (brown coat) hardened, but not too much, we had lunch; then we came back to put on the final coat. The plasterer taught his trade.

Mr. Wright liked what he called "sand-float" finish. It was

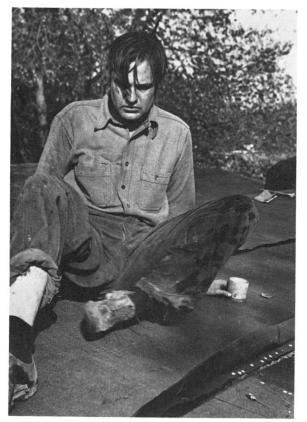

Apprentice William Wesley Peters working on roof.

Apprentices Tafel and John Howe, at Taliesin.

done by placing a piece of carpet over a "float" or trowel, running it over the surface in circular sweeps. The sand would come to the surface. Mr. Wright came by to see if we were doing it right—he was always coming by—and while we floated he told us how he "invented" putting colors into the final coat. In earlier days he used blues, umbers, and yellows mixed together—he changed the proportions depending on what light the surface got—and when the mixture dried, the wall needed no paint. Mr. Wright really hated paint.

Paint was on the surface, not part of structure. He told us how the painters' union had insisted that the painters put the color in the mud, how he'd fought them. He wound up by complaining that the unions cost clients money, what a scourge they were, on and on, while we floated. We learned by doing—the Taliesin way—and by listening.

When the bulk of the apprentices arrived, weeks later—including a couple of young women—I was an old hand. The new arrivals got the impression that I'd been there for years as I showed them how to set studs, nail lath, mix mud, float. . . . My early days in the carpentry and printshops at school, working puppets, working in summer theater, all helped in this first try at supervising construction.

As first arrivals, we got into the drafting room first, doing drawings of the rooms being built as well as renderings of the Imperial Hotel. In the corner of the studio was a photo file crammed with folders showing Mr. Wright's work—the Oak Park buildings, the Prairie houses, and others that came later. I made a list and, early in November, begged off for a couple of days and went to the Chicago area to have a look.

Mr. Wright, with apprentices, at picnic. From left:
Eugene Masselink, Mr. Wright's secretary and artist;
Masselink's brother on a visit; Fritz Benedict; Wes Peters.

3

t wasn't quite "Architecture" that died, but the Chicago commercial style which lost its impetus and fell out of favor. A new breed of "cultured" client opted for more ornament and less functional severity. Sullivan's own popularity, too, began to fade after his last courageous stand against classicism. As the year 1900 approached, change followed change, ever more quickly.

The tremendously exciting spirit in the American heartland had lasted scarcely a generation. The country was still growing, and soon Chicago would be known merely as the Midwest, an intermediate territory, while the real West pushed closer and closer to the Rockies and the Pacific.

With the progression of time and culture, the inevitable "enlightenment" overtook Chicago—and the subsequent "fall." Currents shifted after the turn of the century, communication and travel increased, as did personal wealth. Chicago grew out of her bold, naïve, and provincial personality. Social polish began to glitter with more traditional sparkle, and social acceptance meant social conformity. With the solid comforts of the East dangled before its eyes, the Midwest succumbed again to Eastern values and symbols, smothering most of its own initial sparks of individuality. It was predictable that, once "enlightened," the Midwest became uncomfortably aware of its lack of refinement and developed a long-lasting inferiority complex toward the East. And Europe.

In its enthusiasm and haste to acquire at least the superficial aspects of the East, the Midwest snatched here and there at every representation of culture, ending up with a ludicrous mélange of styles and tastes, in architecture as in everything else. In a much broader sense, it is clear that with the first World War came a new era of thinking and feeling that totally swept away any remnants of the frontier spirit in America and brought the entire world abruptly into a fully modern era.

No, "Architecture" did not die. Before the turn of the century, there was still enough of the open-plains spirit of freedom left in Chicago to cause something new to spring up—a wholly original, unprecedented, practical, satisfying *residential architecture*. Sullivan and his colleagues, who were busy designing high-rise metal frame giants, gave little thought to houses for the people who worked in these buildings. Sullivan, in fact, was so bored by residential architecture that he gave the few house commissions that came into the office to his ambitious young draftsman—F. L. Wright (which is how he signed drawings at this time)—to do after office hours. The work was a blessing, for Wright got to know his clients intimately as he designed their houses.

Soon, neighbors of F. L. Wright in Oak Park began to engage him directly to design houses. He had married at twenty-two and already his family was growing, so he needed to stretch his finances by taking on extra work. He designed several houses on the side, without telling Sullivan, who had tremendous affection for Mr. Wright, for his spirit and inquisitiveness. Sullivan, who had no children of his own, had a fatherly attitude toward his young draftsman. And Wright must have felt guilty about accepting outside work, since his formal contract with Adler and Sullivan specifically prohibited his doing so. Therefore, he attached the name of a friend, another young architect, to several jobs.

Mr. Wright often talked about his moonlighting projects— "bootlegged," as he called them—to us in the Fellowship. In his mid-sixties, he'd look back at what he'd done when he was twenty-two, fairly amused at himself. He always said he'd let down *Lieber Meister*—which is how he referred to Sullivan—and that he felt bad about it.

He often told this story: One day Sullivan was riding through town, on the way to the office, in a buggy. Passing a lot where foundations were being laid, he recognized the style immediately. His feelings were stung and his Irish temper flared. He came into the office and stormed over to Mr. Wright, saying he'd seen the foundation and knew whose it was. Without waiting for an explanation, he roared out, "Wright, you're fired." The *Lieber Meister* and the devoted follower separated

Sullivan's Charnley house, Astor Street, Chicago, designed by Mr. Wright when he worked as a draftsman at Adler and Sullivan.

Frank Lloyd Wright studio in Oak Park—sculpture integrated with architecture.

with harsh words. Their mutual silence lasted a dozen years.

The story in the *Autobiography* is a little different. There Mr. Wright says that Sullivan learned about his extra-office projects and was offended, feeling that Wright had broken his contract with the firm. Sullivan told Wright that his sole interest should be in the Sullivan office while their agreement was in force. Wright asked Adler to intercede for him, something he had never done before, which only further infuriated Sullivan. *Lieber Meister* grew cool and "haughty," and one day Mr. Wright, as he described it, threw down his pencil and made an exit, never to return. Whichever is the truer version, the episode had a definite effect on Mr. Wright. From then on, in his own practice, there was never the slightest hesitation about firing someone, whether it be recalcitrant draftsman, contractor, or client.

Mr. Wright told us this story about Sullivan often. In fact, one of the hardest things at Taliesin was hearing him repeat a story for the twelfth time and trying to respond as if it were a new story. He probably even knew he was repeating himself, but for him each retelling was like reliving history.

Years later I realized how Mr. Wright must have felt about the Adler and Sullivan incident. It must have been in my third year of the Fellowship, just before the Johnson Wax Building. In New York, visiting my folks, I did a few days' work in the office of an architect friend. He needed some extra assistance, and I certainly needed the money. Shortly after I got back to Taliesin, Mr. Wright found out about this work indirectly and, calling it "treason," told me it might be better if I left the Fellowship. My stomach fell, but I stood before him and said, "Do you mean that I should leave immediately, sir?" "Well, Edgar," he said, "why don't you think it over and we'll talk about it again in a week." The week went by, and I went back and asked if he'd thought about it further. He explained that he understood, since he'd been through it himself. He told the Sullivan story again. I listened again—and I stayed. All of us at Taliesin had read the *Autobiography* many times. We knew the stories by heart and how to touch his sympathies.

Even in his young days, Mr. Wright did not have the personality to sit quietly in a corner. Soon after finding the position as detailer with Adler and Sullivan, he knew all the young architects in town worth knowing and within a few years emerged naturally as their most articulate and forceful spokesman and the sharpest designer among them. In the large downtown studios shared by these progressive young men, inexhaustible debates centered on the latest expressions of residential architecture and, in particular, the relationship of form and function.

Guided by Sullivan's ideas, more than by his buildings, and fired by F. L. Wright's extraordinary clear new concepts about the inside and outside of a house, the young people who were to

Wright home and studio, Oak Park, Illinois.

become known as the Prairie School began to shape their ideas. Many of them came to work in the Wright studio in Oak Park.

Even so, Mr. Wright was not actually a member of the Prairie School. A leader, yes, but he could no sooner belong to any school than he could belong to the Elks. The group defined their architectural approach, their beliefs and theories about design—not just for houses, but also for civic and religious buildings. They kept their independence and resisted joining forces with the A.I.A. (American Institute of Architects), which they called retrogressive, Eastern, and uncreative. Theirs was an architectural philosophy that covered everything. The Prairie architects identified with the simplification and practicality of the Chicago School's commercial structures, but turned their sights for the time being to smaller-scale architecture.

Why should it be that suddenly an entire generation of regional architects turned their interest to designing houses? How did the traditional passion for designing monuments, cathedrals, government buildings, and grand mansions lose its partisans? Elaborate structures became too expensive. People grew tired of them.

After several centuries of increasingly rich and indigestible architectural styles, there was an outcry by the late 1860s for a return to simplicity and purity, both in architecture and in the design of furnishings. There was a new clamor for honesty in production techniques and honesty in the use of materials. The Arts and Crafts movement, the British project for reform led by William Morris, was the first group to speak out clearly against the overblown Victorian vulgarity of tasteless industrialization. Within a short time, the ideas of the Arts and Crafts movement traveled to America and took hold in Chicago. Hull House, founded by Jane Addams toward the very end of the century, is the best known center for the activities of the movement. It was here in 1901 that Wright gave his famous lecture "The Art and Craft of the Machine," where he welcomed the new technological age, envisioning a modern beauty growing out of the machine and man's control of it.

The Arts and Crafts movement in England was concerned with a return to the quality of work handcrafted by artisans in the old tradition. In the United States it acknowledged the future rather than the past and emphasized both the simple machine streamline and the unpretentious qualities of folk crafts and primitive house design. These less sophisticated arts became familiar through articles in the popular homemaker magazines.

Women, now, were starting to have a voice in the design of homes and household devices. By the end of the nineteenth century, women had become household managers, running home and budget with common sense and practicality. Curiously, though, as their needs were more carefully considered by the architects, women themselves twisted back to Victorian views.

Housewives had clamored for better-planned interior space, easier maintenance, more logical work areas. And yet, when the Prairie house offered these improvements, they accused the style of being harsh and masculine and retreated to a vision of themselves as lovely ladies and *grandes dames* in an atmosphere of fluff and painted decoration and curlicues. Women were still plagued by a dual identification, and they fell back on the image of frills. No architect could put an honest and practical Prairie interior in an overblown Victorian container.

Exemplified most eloquently by Wright, what the Prairie School offered in its early years was a fundamental change in the exterior and interior of the house. Historical styles without and traditional arrangements within were emphatically discarded. The new Prairie house sat close to the ground, spreading its lines of strong horizontality like space anchors to the site. Mr. Wright often said, "Out of the ground and into the light." The materials defining the exterior were direct statements and looked like what they were: natural brick, or wood and stucco. The houses presented sharp, boldly geometric lines to the eye, uncluttered by scrolls or arabesques or any other traditional jigsaw finery. Not that the Prairie house designers flatly rejected all ornaments as out of keeping with the new style—but they created ornament by textures and colors, or by the nature of the materials themselves, or by the different elements that made up the total mass. Echoes of the intricately beautiful system of organic ornament that Sullivan had used in his skyscrapers appeared in some of the Prairie houses, more subtle and ever appropriate. Honest grace and charm.

The true revolution of the Prairie house was not so much in simplification and emphatic horizontality, but in the way interior space was planned. Often it was done in such a subtle way that the clients were not aware of a new environment reshaping their most basic living patterns.

For centuries and centuries, the house had been a large box broken up into small box-rooms, not very comfortable, not very practical without servants, and laid out with almost no regard for actual human needs and patterns of living. A house has to be much more than a well-proportioned container divided up into other mathematically regulated compartments. The house needed to be broken open, relaxed, humanized. And at a time of rising land and building costs, decreasing family size, less available permanent domestic help, and new technology and industrial advances familiar to everyone, the American house was due for some very important changes.

"The American house lies," Mr. Wright used to tell us. It had no sense of unity, no sense of space. In his Sunday lectures to the Fellowship, or in the course of everyday work in the drafting room at Taliesin, Mr. Wright kept reminding us that a house becomes more a home by being a work of art. This spirit took hold of all the apprentices who were truly sympathetic to his philosophy. He called the average house a bedeviled box, with holes. The holes were trimmed. Bastardized to the last, everything in the house got painted or, on the inside, varnished, to reduce the natural materials to something other than themselves.

In talking about his early philosophy of house design, and organic architecture in general, Mr. Wright would always describe the "destruction of the box." He would draw us a box, thus:

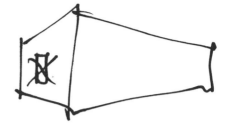

Then he'd put in a couple of holes for doors and windows:

And he'd explain that—according to the principles of engineering that every architect has to know—the most economic support of the building is not at the corners but at a certain distance in from the corners. Like this:

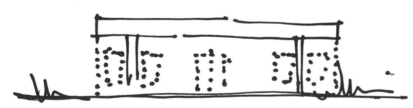

This short space, from the supporting wall out to the unsupported corner, is cantilever. That is easy to understand today, because we are all accustomed to seeing dramatic cantilevers working in large-scale buildings. But when Mr. Wright knocked the corners out of the box and thereby created a cantilever—that was revolution!

What happens when the corners are removed from a building? In the first place, the boxiness disappears. There is a new feeling of *continuous space*. Walls? They no longer serve as barriers, keeping the inside of the box in and the outside world out. They become screens, letting inside out and outside in. We apprentices must have heard this a thousand times. Each time it sounded truer.

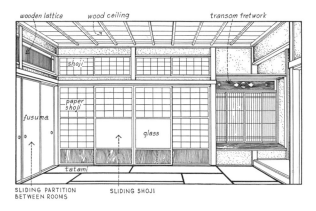

wooden lattice   wood ceiling   transom fretwork

shoji

paper shoji

fusuma   glass

tatami

SLIDING PARTITION   SLIDING SHOJI
BETWEEN ROOMS

Sometimes Mr. Wright would use the example of Japanese architecture to illustrate his point. The Japanese house, with its sliding screens, gives a unique sense of movable space. With each rearrangement of the screens, we become aware of the *shape of the space* or, like the Japanese print, of merely an interruption of space, a moment in space. Another dimension, he called it. Imagine the surprise he experienced when, by chance, he came across a quotation from Lao-tzu: "The reality of the building does not consist in the four walls and the roof but in the space within to be lived in."

Mr. Wright felt great affinity for Japanese culture and had a deep understanding of it. He had visited Japan before his Imperial Hotel in Tokyo was even a dream. He wore Japanese clothing and wandered throughout the countryside, experiencing to the fullest this ancient culture.

He had a passion for the woodblock prints, and his taste was very much respected by dealers in Japan. He loved the porcelain and the fine carved figurines and brought many magnificent pieces back with him. Taliesin, while we were there, was filled with a remarkable oriental collection, indoors and out. He was already familiar with Japanese prints, which were becoming fashionable to collect. However, Mr. Wright's major exposure to Japanese architecture must have been at the World's Columbian Exposition of 1893, where the Japanese government had a fascinating, curiosity-catching exhibit on a little island in an artificial lake, reached by a wooden bridge. This was the Ho-o-den, a half-size reproduction of an existing wooden temple.

In later years, Mr. Wright denied vociferously—perhaps too vociferously— that this pavilion and Japanese architecture in general had ever had any influence on his own work. He acknowledged, though, the philosophical, theoretical influence of the Japanese approach—its pared-down quality, intense simplification, and "organic character."

Whether due to unconscious reflection of Japanese style or artistic coincidence, there are clear parallels between Japanese dwellings and Mr. Wright's idea of the Prairie house. The most prominent similarities are horizontality and the fact that the house hugs the earth. Inside, the sliding panels of different degrees of translucency in the Japanese house give a sense of open space like the effects achieved by Mr. Wright's open floor plan. The Japanese house is traditionally based on a three-foot by six-foot

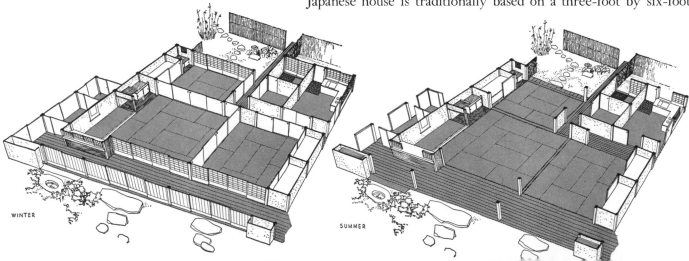

WINTER   SUMMER

module that provides a subtle overall organization. This is the size of the tatami mats used to cover the floor. Mr. Wright experimented with different kinds of modular systems, using them as organizational bases in his earliest houses.

After Mr. Wright had explained how the corners of the box would be done away with, he would ask us, "Why can't the same thing happen in other planes, for instance at the junction of wall and ceiling? If it works in the horizontal, it should work in the vertical." But this wasn't actually tested until he designed the Johnson Wax Building in 1936.

Now that Mr. Wright had thoroughly revolutionized the basic shape of the house, he explained to us in detail each innovation planned to make the house work as a totality. He started at the top and the bottom of the house at the same time. Got rid of the attic, "useless dead space," and the basement, "more wasteful space." Wes Peters used to say, not altogether seriously, that if Mr. Wright had invented attics and cellars he would have called them the greatest of all contributions to "the house."

"But Mr. Wright," one of us asked, "what about storage?" "Closets?" he answered, "they're nothing but unsanitary boxes! And as for your storage, there's no reason for people to hold on to so much junk!" By eliminating the basement wherever he could, especially in later houses, Mr. Wright created a new personality for the structure. He made it grow right out of the ground. He wanted the house to sit firmly *on* the ground, not to look half-buried *in* it. The foundations projected only slightly above the earth, creating the visual effect of a platform for the building above.

One of Mr. Wright's broadest concerns in rethinking the house was how to create the feeling of comfortable shelter. That, after all, is what architecture is all about. To reinforce the sense of security in the building achieved by horizontal lines and solid placement on the earth, Mr. Wright flattened the sharply gabled roof. He reduced it to a nearly flat roof or sometimes to a completely flat one, spreading out like a broad, protective brow over the house.

Nestling low on the roof was to be a wide, strong-looking chimney, indicative of the large fireplace that would provide a focal point for the interior. A real fireplace now, not a Victorian mantelpiece with a mirror above and a fancy screen below. Mr. Wright intended the hearth to serve as a meeting place for the family, always saying, "The hearth is the center of the home." This was an example of the way he consciously attempted to direct and organize the patterns of family living.

In keeping with his idea of walls as screens, Mr. Wright gave the outside surfaces of the house a new meaning. The wall started at the foundation platform and rose in an undisturbed line up to the sills of the second-story windows. It didn't go all the way up and hit against the underside of the roof, like the side of a

Frederick G. Robie house, Chicago, Illinois, 1906.

box. The bands of windows on the upper story lightened the entire house, and the gently sloping roof threw its eaves out over the windows, letting light reflect back softly. There is always a certain warmth inside a Wright house, like a soft halo, caused by the way the sun hits the ground and is reflected back up again on the soffit. You never get this kind of glow from a Bauhaus house.

Inside, Mr. Wright made one extensive change that affected every physical element—as well as the impressions and reactions of every person who entered the house: He changed the scale and brought it down to his own human reference. He often used to tell us, paraphrasing his own essay on house building: "I took the human being, at five feet eight and one-half inches tall, like myself, as the human scale. If I had been taller, the scale might have been different."

Since the ancients, architecture had been traditionally governed by a scale that operated according to rational systems on paper, based on mathematics or physics or philosophy, but certainly not on human proportions. Usually, the bigger the building, the bigger the scale, so that it was possible, for example, to have a doorway twelve or fifteen feet high in a large building.

When we talk of a building in human scale, we mean that architect has designed it to make human beings and familiar objects appear of normal size when seen inside and near by. Even if a building is extremely large, sensitive detailing on both exterior and interior will keep it in human scale. Although the people who use the building may not consciously be aware of this, the architect has carefully designed ceiling heights, door and window sizes, stair proportions, placement of switches and handles, and an infinity of other details to fall within the range of familiar experience. That way, users of the building are never overpowered by monumentality or made to feel like giants in a dollhouse.

In every building he designed, whether it was a budget house for a small family or an office building for several thousand employees, Mr. Wright kept the entire structure to "human scale." In fact, the relatively small scale he used causes some problems today, since the average height of Americans has increased considerably since his Oak Park days.

Someone once remarked to him, "Whenever I walk into one of your buildings, the doorways are so low my hat gets knocked off." Mr. Wright merely suggested, "Take you hat off when you come into a house." While I was at the Fellowship, the tallest apprentice around was Wes Peters, six feet and four inches. Mr. Wright never let him forget about his height, since both Wes and the Taliesin ceilings were six feet four. Occasionally, when we gathered in one of the rooms at Taliesin, Mr. Wright would roar out at Wes, "Sit down, Wes! You're destroying the scale!"

This reduction to a more natural scale had the broadest

effect on residential design, but Mr. Wright also developed another design element that has today become commonplace and expected—the open floor plan. He destroyed the boxes on the inside of the box. On the main floor (which was sometimes on the ground level and sometimes a story above), he eliminated partitions and doors designed to isolate and to hide. Open up the house, bring the family together, make living more relaxed. The formality of the dining room was banished, with one large space gently screened into areas for dining, for reading, and for socializing. Windows were lowered, but there were more of them, so the house became brighter, cheerier. Be one with nature outside. Broad horizontal bands around the uppermost parts of the walls made the ceiling appear to settle down intimately over the room, yet the bands of windows gave the rooms an airy and spacious feeling.

Every element was changing. No house had ever been built this way, to express these ideas. Many people in Chicago ridiculed the Prairie house, found derogatory names for it, thought both architect and client were mad. To say nothing of the builders' opinions. Mr. Wright was a young man then, in his twenties, but he carried with him the certainty of greatness. (He used to tell us that if music were his field, he'd be as great as Beethoven!) Some people hate greatness and individuality, resent these qualities, and that is one thing Mr. Wright had to fight all his life. It was especially true with the builders. Like a lot of other people, builders resist doing anything that hasn't been done before. They're afraid to experiment—it costs money. Mr. Wright often said there's nothing so timid as money.

Our own architectural education is in many ways responsible for this dulled attitude. Even today there are many self-appointed eclectics who'd prefer to teach an approved rehash of what's already been built—say, a reproduction of Europe's Mies, or of Le Corbusier, or of Gropius, rather than try something that's appropriate to time, place, and nature. It's my conviction that the most difficult thing for the accomplished architect, no matter what "school" of architectural thinking he follows, is to design what's appropriate at the right setting and the right circumstance. The world over, we see the followers of the best-known architects trying to reflect what they think their masters would have designed for a given problem. The masters cannot be second-guessed, for they too can be wrong. No wonder these followers are often dashed when the client isn't responsive and says he isn't getting a sincere and suitable architectural solution. Too often, the professors are afraid to find out that they've been wrong, afraid they may lose their grip or their jobs. So they decide it's safer to teach what's already been accepted, particularly by the press. This thinking certainly is not limited to today. Mr. Wright came up against it in 1893, and we apprentices had faced it in our own pre-Wright education.

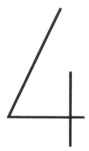

4

Oak Park. Suburb, west of Chicago. Formerly flat farmland. Edge of the prairie. First stop out on the new commuter line.

In the 1880s, when Frank Lloyd Wright moved to Oak Park with his mother and sister, it was a growing community. Quiet, still green, broad streets lined with young trees. They called it "Saint's Rest" because it had so many churches. And so many Unitarians. Plenty of potential clients for a young Unitarian architect. Escape from the evils of the city, from the din and the shuffle, is nothing new.

Nearly a hundred years ago, when young Frank Wright looked around Oak Park, he described the "good people most of whom had taken asylum there to bring up their children in comparative peace, safe from the poisons of the great city." He knew they'd soon build more houses, churches, libraries, banks, sports clubs. Good place to set up a practice.

Oak Park at the turn of the century became more than a prosperous community. Now, it's a staid town, known all over the world, where you expect every other residence to be a Prairie house. The town today has over twenty houses designed by Mr. Wright.

With sometimes eight, ten, twelve, fifteen projects all going at once in those days, Mr. Wright must have had a time taking care of all his clients—running to look at one site, planning for another, holding clients' hands and making each one feel attended to. And also trying to collect fees to keep his own large household and office running. Unpaid salaries and unpaid bills were usual. He cut quite a figure in the town, for he was handsome and always dressed in fine clothing, though his manner of dress was considered rather eccentric. On Sundays, he galloped around the town on horseback. Riding was his main recreation besides singing in the church choir and organizing picnics. His hair was long.

Oak Park is more than a name that you meet on a map or in a book. To get the town's true flavor—in the days when Mr. Wright was its leading personality—you have to stop by the Wright studio, now open to the public. Try to imagine the life once within, hear the neighborhood children shouting, listen to the respectable hum of the successful Protestant community, then walk down the broad streets and experience the complete setting. The mixture of styles is striking—nineteenth-century Victorian beside twentieth-century Prairie style, English half-timber beside colonial. That's American culture—freedom of choice, good, bad, or indifferent, so long as the bank will mortgage.

If you happen to be in Chicago and go out to see the Wright houses in Oak Park—or if you are in Buffalo or Los Angeles or near Pittsburgh—how would you approach a Wright building? What would you look for? You might wonder what the houses meant to the community when they were originally built and how the neighbors reacted to them. You might ask what sort of people they were, the clients who commissioned genius from Mr. Wright. How they looked at the buildings then. More important, you'd ask yourself what these buildings mean today, how we see them and understand them.

First of all, as you approach a building, whether it's a house or a skyscraper or a church, ask why it's there. What is its purpose, its function? Unless it was built as a state capitol or a post office, or for some obvious purpose, it's often difficult to tell what a building is for. What makes a building look like a library, for instance, or a museum? That is, what kind of images do we have about certain types of buildings?

Then, determine what the site's like—what kinds of buildings are nearby, whether there's much street traffic, if the views are pleasant, if the neighborhood is noisy or quiet, what kinds of people are there. Look around. Notice if there are any trees or open spaces. How does the building sit on its site? Does it fit in with the surrounding buildings or does it stand out against them?

As you examine it, decide if it looks comfortable, as though it belongs there. What kind of impression does it create?

Typical street scenes, Oak Park and River Forest.

53

Power? Calm? Repose? Elegance? Simplicity? Does the building convey a sense of unity and organization? Forget what the professional critic may have said about the building. Look at it through your own eyes.

Look at the building carefully to see what it's made of—and how it's made. Try to identify the materials and see how well they are being used. Do they all seem to fit together in harmony? Are they used with understanding and care?

Once you have an overall impression, move closer to the building, taking in details. Let your eye go over individual elements on the exterior—doors and windows, how the height from one floor to the next is stated, what kind of ornament is used, how the sun hits certain angles and how it's reflected or casts shadows. Examine the quality of workmanship. See what sort of planting is used around the building.

After that, focus on the entrance. Notice if it's in the center, off-center, to one side. Ask yourself why it attracts your attention. What does it say as you approach it from the street? Is it inviting? Or is it hidden, perhaps forbidding-looking, indicating privacy?

When you're inside, can you tell immediately if the spaces and style are what you expected after seeing the outside? Analyze your impressions to see whether the building expresses charm and grace. Is the interior a comfortable space to be in? Or is it something you could get accustomed to being comfortable in?

Look around and notice if there are any changes in ceiling heights or in floor levels. Do the volumes flow, or are the spaces cut up and boxed in? Be aware of interesting details that make you take notice of the way the building is put together and how it affects you. Determine the basic forms or elements of the building and watch for changes or variations in them. While you're walking from one area to another, ask yourself if you can feel that someone cared in arranging the total space, as well as the subspaces and details. In other words, can you feel the designer's presence and sense a special personality? If you can't, why not?

After you've been in the building for a while, looking at it carefully and reviewing your impressions, you may want to retrace your steps and look at it all over again. Or you may feel you want to get out as fast as possible. Or perhaps you will want just to linger and feel the building all around you. Do you sense that there is something more to be seen? Think about it. Have you experienced an architectural symphony? A jazzy jazz band? Or dull "canned" music?

Then, sometime later, come back to visit. Suddenly, you see things you didn't catch the first time—and have a new set of responses. What happens to your original impressions? Are they reaffirmed? Do you walk away, finally, thinking, "That building is really a great experience!"?

One time we asked Mr. Wright how he felt when he saw an ugly building. He said, "It makes my teeth hurt."

Frank Lloyd Wright had not been in Oak Park long when, still working as a detailer with Louis Sullivan, he married a redheaded, strong-willed girl, bought a lot near the edge of town, and built his own house. It was strictly an economy building with wood frame and ordinary brick. Like most architects, he added to his house when he got some money—and kept adding. His family expanded and crowded him out of his upstairs drafting room, so he built a vast playroom for the six children and a separate studio for himself next door, where he hoped to be able to work in peace, away from the noise and household mess. Just to keep in touch, he also maintained an office in downtown Chicago.

Among his neighbors, the Wright studio was always referred to as "the house with the tree through the roof" because of the opening cut through the library ceiling to let a willow grow uninterrupted. The studio was a highly personal expression of the artist in Wright. The library, the study, and the two-story drafting room were comfortable spaces in which to work, decorated with Japanese prints and his own architectural drawings and always filled with flowers or greens. Light flooded into the work space from high above. Artwork was built into the exterior of the studio, white sculpted figures, all precast, on either side of the entrance. Here, Mr. Wright was trying out his theories on himself, searching to incorporate the arts with architecture for a greater whole. Architecture, to him, was always the "mother art," and the other arts were forever subservient. With these sculptures, and later with sculptures at Midway Gardens and abstract stonework at the Imperial Hotel, Mr. Wright waged a constant battle with sculptors, telling them where, when, and how to do what.

Even as early as 1893, Mr. Wright had begun to use low, broad urns or "pots" in the composition of his house design, placing them at terminal positions along low walls. One of Sullivan's mottoes, which Mr. Wright took to heart, was "Take care of the terminal and the rest will take care of itself." His use of the urn was copied by other Prairie School architects until it became their symbol. Even today, the urn is the emblem for the *Prairie School Review.* In his later years at Taliesin, Mr. Wright placed a piece of sculpture or a Ming vase or some other work of art at every turning, every corner.

Whether the Prairie style would have developed as it did without the Winslow house, it's hard to say, but this was the forerunner of the strong, sophisticated Oak Park homes. It was also Frank Wright's first independent commission after he left Adler and Sullivan in 1893 and opened his own office, with a friend, downtown in the Schiller Building. William H. Winslow, whom young Wright knew through the Winslow Orna-

William H. Winslow house, River Forest, Illinois, 1893. *Porte-cochère* at left was designed for horse and buggy. The walls under the broad eaves are highly decorated. In describing the house, Mr. Wright used to say it was the last time he used double-hung windows and that this house set the bungalow style in the United States. *"Bungala,"* in Hindi, means house.

mental Iron Works, wanted a house in River Forest, just beyond Oak Park. He was a musician, an inventor, and a successful businessman who was fascinated by new steam automobiles, photography, and the latest in printing processes. His choice of the twenty-six-year-old Wright as architect was in keeping with the rest of his modern, but not avant-garde, tastes. As often happened with Mr. Wright and his clients, their relationship extended beyond the bounds of the commission at hand. Winslow and Mr. Wright later collaborated on the private publication of a book produced on a basement printing press. For years, the Wrights joined the Winslow family at picnics and holiday dinners.

Wright's design of the Winslow house provoked lively reactions around the suburb. Mr. Winslow and his new home became the subjects of local debates on style and taste. The house was admired by many modern-thinking, middle-class businessmen, and Frank Wright soon found dozens of clients coming

to his door. He never solicited.

In the front portion of the Winslow house, facing the street, Mr. Wright kept a degree of formality. The setting for the entrance and the front door itself are reminiscent of Louis Sullivan's ornament—Mr. Wright could by this time produce the Sullivan style to perfection. The ornament on the door is so spontaneous and free-flowing that the carver's chisel could roam around on the wood. Winslow, who made cabinets in his spare time, appreciated his architect's sensitivity to the qualities of wood. Winslow was well known for architectural iron and brass work, so Mr. Wright designed an ornamental fence with his client's product on one side of the house. No function. Just to be ornamental. The garage floor was a turntable—to turn the car around!

At the rear of the house, away from public view, Mr. Wright expressed a completely different feeling. Here he was less strict and formal. He abandoned the symmetry of the front, so

that the differentiated forms of the house began to reveal how interior spaces were arranged—the tall angled stair tower with its long narrow windows, the rounded swell at the end of the dining room with a curved band of leaded glass windows, the bedroom above protected by a broad sweep of roof. The richness of texture here, the variety of forms, the complexity of "composition," point to a new and more highly evolved concept of the house. Form expressing function.

Frank Lloyd Wright was proud of his design and, like any artist proud of his work—especially a first masterpiece—he signed it. Down in the lower right corner as you face the side entrance, incised in the stone base, is a little symbol: a square enclosing a cross within a circle. This emblem was simplified, in the next few years, until it became the symbol associated with Mr. Wright throughout his career: a red square. It is not common practice for an architect to put his emblem on a building, but Mr. Wright wanted to sign his buildings as he signed his drawings.

The house is "signed" with the emblem Mr. Wright used then, a cross surrounded by a circle in a square. His "logo" later became a red square.

By 1902, the design of the Ward Willits and Heurtley houses had begun to articulate a style, an organization of the architectural elements that we now recognize as his own Prairie style, which culminates with the Robie, Coonley, and Little houses. Here, clearly and forcefully, is Mr. Wright's revolution in architectural space—free-flowing yet interpenetrating interiors, the play of interlocking horizontal forms with their vertical counterpoint reflected on the exterior, the dissolution of indoors to outdoors, outdoors to indoors. Though almost no true Prairie houses were designed after about 1914, the architectural philosophy that generated them is a main thread of the continuity that runs through the seventy years of Mr. Wright's career.

Each house had its scenario. One of the first Oak Park clients, a lawyer, came to Mr. Wright one day and said he wanted a Wright house, but not like the house designed for Winslow—he didn't want to be a laughingstock.

Many years later, Mr. Wright himself did just that. There are some buildings of his that he didn't quite disown, but that he really didn't like. He'd cross the street, even go around the block, to avoid seeing them. To satisfy his lawyer client and, as he always emphasized, to make some money to clothe his children properly, Mr. Wright designed a house for Nathan Moore: English half-timber. He said his heart wasn't in it and he always referred to it with embarrassment, but it doesn't seem as if he could have been ill at ease with a house into which he'd put so much care and detail. The most remarkable thing is that when he redesigned the house after a fire in 1922, Mr. Wright went back to extremely Sullivanesque detail in the terra-cotta and wood carving. The Moore house is sheer delight, the only English half-timber house with a porch and second-floor terrace—a lesson for the English.

Top: Garage at right, with Moore house, set tight to the street, in the Oriental urban way. (The garage is the only part of the original house).

Below: Main rooms facing the garden.

Details of various materials in Moore house, second floor
terrace—terra-cotta decoration, cornice decoration,
cornice of stone, slate roof.

Living room fireplace, decorated with wood, and exposed
electric lights. Furniture not designed or selected by
architect.

Chauncey Williams house, River Forest, Illinois.

In the height of his Oak Park days, Frank Lloyd Wright was closely watched by the younger set of Chicago architects. They were as quick to pick up his ideas as he was to create them. Later, when we were all at Taliesin, I remember that whenever he saw a photograph of the Chauncey Williams house, one with a pitched roof that he'd designed in 1895, he would chuckle. He had tried out what he called a Hans Christian Andersen approach, massing big rocks around the base to create the feeling of a house sitting firmly on the ground. But he wasn't satisfied with the effect. It looked fake, contrived, and he never did it again. Meanwhile, architectural copyists around Chicago saw this new trick and picked it up immediately. Mr. Wright would laugh as he told us that the local architects had copied even his mistakes. Some less skillful designers took the Wright forms and simply attached them to the standard Victorian homes with "guillotine" double-hung windows, high-ceilinged rooms, and high doorways, copying—with no understanding—what they thought was fashion. There was no doubt about it: Before he was even forty, Frank Lloyd Wright had become the fashionable architect.

But then what did he do? He dropped everything, turned his back on his practice and his large family, on the successful middle-class life in Oak Park, on the promise of even greater professional popularity and a brilliant career. He fell in love with a client's wife, Mamah Borthwick Cheney, and went off with her to Europe in 1909.

His act may appear self-destructive and more than irresponsible. Yet, in a deep sense, he was crystallizing through his actions the beliefs that had been formulating inside him for years. Although he was completely involved in a conservative middle-class milieu, he had begun to feel a strong need for personal freedom, even if it went counter to social convention. He had to act as he did, not out of impulse or a bohemian attitude of revolt, but out of profound conviction. And he loved Mamah. Explaining his decisions in a letter to his friend and client Francis Little, Mr. Wright wrote in 1911 about so-called principles which he felt were prejudices, about the state of marriage, property, the human soul. He wrote that marriage should be freedom of choice, love in one's heart, that he loved his children, his sisters and aunts and mother, loved his work, and the woman who had chosen to be with him. Lastly, he wrote about the truth in his soul, even going so far as to say there was God in him that commanded him to do what he had done.

When Mr. Wright left for Europe, he was not just running away, he was also going abroad on business. The German publisher Ernst Wasmuth, in Berlin, who was preparing a major monograph on Wright's work, needed his assistance in refining certain drawings for publication. The 1911 *Ausgefuehrte Bauten und Entwuerfe* was an oversized folio of a hundred plates showing both architectural plans and details of ornament. No creative architect of the time missed seeing it. This folio, which solidified the new modern direction, became a reference point for decades of European architecture.

Until Mr. Wright's departure for Europe, his Oak Park studio remained the vibrant center of Chicago architecture. Many of the city's progressive young architects, already graduates and accomplished professionals, came to work and learn by practice and observation. Marion Mahony, Walter Burley Griffin, and William Drummond were among them. Mr. Wright claimed he wasn't a teacher, but he usually took in a few young apprentices just the same; he liked to have spirited young people around him. This was in keeping with the atelier system of architecture, which was still generally accepted. Even so, the organization and function of the studio were quite unlike the Taliesin Fellowship later.

Taliesin was to be a self-sufficient, self-contained total community, much more than an architect's office. The studio, on the other hand, operated as a business, drafting and preparing the more personalized renderings for presentation to clients or for exhibition and publication. Nevertheless, the studio had a very special and individualized atmosphere, since Mr. Wright always created his own world wherever he was—whether it was Oak Park, the Arizona desert, downtown Tokyo, or the Plaza Hotel in New York. His personality swept everyone in, conquering by charm as much as by strength, and the Oak Park studio, like any of his later bases, was business office and artist's atelier and family home. People who worked for him were absorbed into all the facets of his life. These young architects somehow bore the imprint of the Wright style, though it worked out in different ways, with some content to copy, others to deny the style later and turn to more traditional forms, and others to develop their own styles based on Mr. Wright's new concepts of space and materials. During his absence in Europe, young architects who had been associated with the studio had a chance to work out their own ideas in architecture and establish contacts with their own potential clients. While Mr. Wright was busy in Germany and Italy, the young Prairie School really came into its own.

By the time he returned to Chicago in 1911 with Mamah Borthwick Cheney, his practice and his position in the community had changed. Many of us at Taliesin later speculated that if Mr. Wright hadn't gone to Europe in 1909, he would have established himself as the Midwest's most popular architect. But then again, you can't tell. He never would toe the mark. Just when you got to expect one thing, he'd do another. And while the nature of his practice did change after the time he spent in Europe, the publications resulting from that long stay abroad made him more influential and respected in Germany, Austria, and the Netherlands than he was to be in his own country for many decades.

From time to time we apprentices at Taliesin made pilgrimages to Oak Park or other suburbs around Chicago to see the great prairie houses. When we told Mr. Wright of our plans, he was always delighted, for he loved his houses like his own children. One such visit took place my first Thanksgiving at Taliesin. A fellow apprentice invited me to his family's home in suburbia for the holiday—a novel experience for a New Yorker. The quiet calm of Main Street, the self-satisfied atmosphere of the best streets on the right side of the railroad.

On the way back to Taliesin, we stopped in Oak Park for the day. Mr. Wright had told us which houses to see. We developed a technique for getting inside. At each house we rang the doorbell like salesmen and greeted the inhabitants by saying, "Hello! We're students from Taliesin and we'd like to tell Mr. Wright we saw the inside of your house." We weren't always successful.

Even then, owners of Wright houses were subjected to endless visits by students and devoted Wright enthusiasts. When we returned from River Forest, or Oak Park, or Riverside, Mr. Wright would listen to our stories briefly. Then he'd tell us stories. He had an anecdote for every house; it was uncanny how sharply the details remained in his memory. He delighted in creating vignettes about the clients. "Mrs. Client was always a lady," he'd say. Or, "She dyed her hair blue." Or, "She only wore long dresses." There might be a story, too, about a contractor—villainous member of what Mr. Wright called the "unholy trinity"—architect, client, and contractor. I began to realize—through these stories—that every architectural episode in Mr. Wright's life had to have a villain—and it was usually the contractor.

No building moved ahead until the villain was established and it was best not to change villains in mid-building. Of course, the contractors probably looked upon Mr. Wright as the villain. He never tired of repeating, "The architect's most effective tools are the eraser in the drafting room and the wrecking bar on the job." When Mr. Wright visited one of his construction sites and saw a wall that was the least bit crooked, he'd grab a wrecking bar and knock the wall down. He abhorred shoddy workmanship. Today architects are not accustomed to dealing directly with workmen. If there's any problem on a job, we notify the superintendent. This is simply one of the basic rules of the trade. The architect does not walk onto the site and pull down a wall. Mr. Wright had his share of troubles with workmen. Once, when he was on a job, a couple of bricks came flying by, barely missing him. No wonder.

But the contractor and workmen weren't the only villains. Sometimes the client's wife was a villain in disguise. Mr. Wright's buildings were always the result of a relationship between men, and Mrs. Client was too often in the way. He often said, "Only fools and women criticize half-done work." Mr. Wright was very serious in the belief that someone was trying to destroy him, that a devil was always lurking behind the scenes.

Occasionally, once the Fellowship was established, visiting architects would ask to see Taliesin. They would come out to meet Mr. Wright, hoping for a personally conducted tour of his best-known Prairie houses and his other buildings in the Chicago area. However, in the early days Mr. Wright—whose opinion of other architects, especially members of the Bauhaus, was very well known—never missed an opportunity to rail at the visitors. He may have demonstrated very little continuity in the way he did things, but he never deviated from his dim appreciation of the "imported" architects. He thought these Internationalists were damaging our country with their functionalism, their infatuation with the machine, and their architectural style that was supposed to fit in anywhere but in truth was at home nowhere. In part, his vehemence was display for the press, maintaining the public image. He always enjoyed a stir.

His attitude was genuine nonetheless. Mr. Wright had berated American taste for reverting to the Beaux-Arts European "style" in the 1893 Exposition; by 1929 he could demonstrate that American architecture, like everything else, had gone bankrupt, sterile. And after the Depression, when the Eastern seaboard decided it could use something architecturally new, did it look to the West of the United States, to its own sons? Certainly not! It went to the Bauhaus.

When the Bauhaus came over from Europe, it wasn't an importation; it was a full-scale invasion of the schools, the architectural magazines, and the press. Bauhaus people favored the "team effort"—planner, designer, architect, engineer, and decorator working as a group. Individual responsibility was gone, sold out to the committee, a hiding place for the usual. And even today, where does the country turn for a shiny new style? Back to Europe—to Europe of fifty years ago.

Mr. Wright liked to tease, but his intent was serious. During the Fellowship, whenever he came back from a trip he'd tell us of jousts with the "outside" architects. In Detroit, for example, he talked with Albert Kahn, prestigious designer of industrial buildings. Kahn said, "Frank, architecture is ninety-five percent business and five percent design." "Then show me your five percent design," shot back Mr. Wright with a characteristic chuckle.

Each time he read that the French architect Le Corbusier had completed a building he would say, "Well, now that he's finished one building, he'll go write four books about it." Then he'd go on about the French. "All they're interested in is fashion," he'd tell us. "Fashion and perfume and sauces. They ruin perfectly good food with their sauces." In the mid-1930s, Le Corbusier came to Madison to speak at the university. Someone from the fine arts department phoned Taliesin, asking for permission to bring "Corbu" for a visit. Mr. Wright replied, "No, I am not interested in meeting Mr. Le Corbusier." Then he came into the drafting room and said to us, "Corbu's influence in this country is just terrible, and he has no business here. I don't want to have to shake his hand." The curious thing is that Mr. Wright credited Le Corbusier with much more success and acceptance than he actually had at that time.

On a trip to New York, Mr. Wright said to architect Corbett, who was mainly responsible for the design of Radio City, "Corbett, you're the best of your crowd." "And Mr. Wright," Corbett replied, "you're the best of yours." Another chuckle.

When Walter Gropius, the German architect and father of the Bauhaus school, was in Madison on a lecture tour, the Corbu story was repeated. There was a call: "Mr. Gropius is here and he would like very much to come out and meet you." Gropius must have been warned what the response was likely to be. Mr. Wright was brusque: "I'm very sorry. I'm quite busy and I have no desire to meet or entertain Herr Gropius. What he stands for and what I stand for are poles apart. Our ideas could never merge. In a sense, we're professional enemies—but he's an outside enemy. At least I'm staying in my own country." We all knew he felt that the European architects were staging a takeover of the profession in America.

It was great overhearing these phone conversations. His office was right next to the drafting room, and we could catch every word. We sat in complete silence whenever there was a call like this. Mr. Wright would then saunter into the drafting room and say triumphantly, "Well, I told him!"

Just after the phone call about Gropius—it was early in the morning—Mr. Wright announced that we were driving to Racine on Johnson Building business. That's how I found out about the trip—ten minutes before we were supposed to leave. We could make it to Racine and back in a day, driving down to Madison and cutting across a few country backroads. Every so often, Mr. Wright would get a strong intuitive feeling to go down and have a look at one of the jobs, to see how it was coming along. Don't call ahead—just go—was his policy If we left Taliesin right after breakfast, we could get to Racine by noon, see the job, and drive back in the evening.

So, early that morning we left in the Lincoln Zephyr, Cherokee red like all his cars. When we got near Madison, he said, "Go to the Jacobs house." This was the first of the 1930s Usonian houses and was well under construction. We parked the car in front, opposite the carport. As we drove up, out came a group of men, walking directly toward our car. They couldn't miss us. In the group was Herr Gropius.

He recognized Mr. Wright at once and came right over.

Mr. Wright inspecting his first use of underfloor piping for radiant heating. Apprentices Thomson and Caraway.

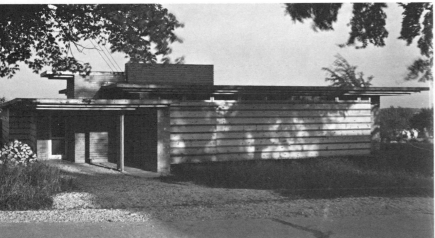

First Jacobs house, seen from garden, 1936, with "carport" (Mr. Wright invented the term).

Left: Second Jacobs house, Middleton, Wisconsin, 1943.

One of the men greeted Mr. Wright and said, "Mr. Wright, this is Dr. Gropius." And Gropius leaned down and said through the open window, "Mr. Wright, it's a pleasure to meet you. I have always admired your work." Mr. Wright, sitting calmly in the front seat, merely turned slightly to face Gropius and said, "Herr Gropius, you're a guest of the university here. I just want to tell you that they're as snobbish here as they are at Harvard, only they don't have a New England accent." Turning to me, he continued jauntily, "Well, we have to get on, Edgar!" That was the signal. I put the car in gear and we were off, leaving Mr. Gropius and colleagues standing there.

Late that afternoon, Mr. Wright decided to drive back through Milwaukee. It was a little out of the way, but he wanted a good dinner and he liked the Old Heidelberg Restaurant there. The restaurant was on a slope. We stopped at the entrance for Mr. Wright to alight. I parked the car in a space behind another car, but forgot to leave it in gear or pull the brake. The two cars were bumper to bumper. When we came out after dinner, our car was gone. But no, there it was, a block away, at the foot of the slope. The owner of the car we leaned against had driven away and the unblocked Zephyr had rolled down the hill, driverless, right into the back of another car. Beyond that car was the river. The owner of the damaged car was stalking around, steaming, looking impatiently for the master of the errant Zephyr. He took Mr. Wright by storm, but Mr. Wright was calm. "It's not my fault," he told the fellow in all seriousness. "If you didn't have your car here in the first place, it wouldn't have got hit." Then, my cue: "Come on, Edgar, let's go. We're needed at Taliesin." And off we went. In his opinion, his car could do no wrong.

After a while he started to have misgivings about his inhospitable behavior toward some European architects. He began welcoming others to Taliesin. In spite of his bluster, he had tender spots. Regularly every weekend, we began having visitors to Taliesin—architects, students, parents of apprentices, artists, local people, and others interested in seeing how the Fellowship lived. Mr. Wright was always utterly charming and cordial, making guests feel at home. Part of his welcome came from a certain social grace, and part was natural Midwestern hospitality. Like the lord of the manor, he took immense pride in showing his domain, explaining, demonstrating as he led people around.

At first we weren't quite sure how to handle these visits, but Mr. Wright settled on a standard visitor's charge (for guests who weren't specifically invited) of fifty cents, children free. Soon after we started charging admission, Mr. Wright also initiated a sign-in guest book, perhaps for a mailing list to advertise his future publications. We apprentices greeted the visitors, took them around through the entrance court, up the hill, and through the drafting room and kitchen area. Later, after we'd completed the rebuilding at Hillside, we'd show them the new theater and drafting room over there. Mr. Wright expected us to keep an eye out for visitors of real substance, interesting in one way or another, and to introduce such people to him. I always tried to escort the colorful or well-known visitors. You could pick them out easily from the gawking farmers who'd been sent by the local people to see what it was like "up to Wright's."

As we took the guests around, Mr. Wright would appraise them from a distance. If they seemed pleasant, he'd nod or sometimes come over and welcome them, chatting in his warmest manner and making them feel comfortable. For us apprentices, the weekend visitors brought a certain relief. We did get tired of each other, living that close. We knew each other's opinions about everything in the world, and all reactions had become predictable. Mr. Wright was equally eager for these weekend breaks. He began to get more and more work, in the middle 1930s, and he also began to invite more people up for the weekends. "Just call," he'd say to visitors when they left on Sunday afternoon. "Call and come out to see us again. We'll get some food from the farm together for you." It was one thing for him to be so gracious, but it was a strain on Mrs. Wright, with guests arriving often and unpredictably. Any day, he might say to her, "Olya, there're twelve people on the way up from Madison for lunch. Put some more water in the soup." "Oh no, Fr-r-r-rank," she'd wail, "we haven't a thing to serve them. I want it to be nice for them." "It'll be nice enough," he'd retort. Nothing ever needed to go smoothly. He didn't believe it should. And Mrs. Wright was the one who had to pick up all the pieces.

A call came one Friday morning from a couple of young Chicago architects who said that the migrated German architect Mies van der Rohe would like to visit Taliesin, Mr. Wright replied, "By all means, bring him up." Mr. Wright had a great deal of respect for Mies' work. He'd seen the Tugendhat house and the Barcelona pavilion in publications, and he viewed Mies as an individualist, not as part of a foreign school or movement.

That Friday, the two men drove Mies up in time for lunch. We were amazed to see Mr. Wright get along with Mies so well. In fact, the afternoon's visit turned into a four-day stay. Mies spent the entire weekend at Taliesin, with a German apprentice on constant duty as interpreter. The two colleagues returned to Chicago, but Mies was promised a ride back to Chicago with Mr. Wright. By the guest's fourth day at Taliesin, Mrs. Wright took a look at him and exclaimed, "Poor Mr. Mies! His white shirt is quite gray!" He'd never planned to stay that long and hadn't brought a change of clothes. Mies was rumpled and ragged.

Mr. Wright, translator in center, Mies at right.
Below: Mies squinting into the sun; myself and translator.

On the way back to Mies' Chicago hotel on Monday, Mr. Wright arranged a grand tour for him—appointing me chauffeur. We drove to Racine first to see the Johnson Wax Building, under construction. The columns and the bridge were already up, and Mr. Wright showed him the building with great pride. All along, Mies had seemed pleased and was being very appreciative of Mr. Wright's attentions, nodding his head and saying *Ja* every so often as he listened to the translated explanations. He was a quiet man, shy and not very communicative who had built an aura around himself.

The greatest difference between Mies and Mr. Wright, we felt, talking it over later, was that while Mies dedicated his entire life to the search for one style, refining and purifying, Mr. Wright kept evolving, growing, and developing new styles. He was never locked into one design establishment, which bore out his favorite phrase: "What we did yesterday, we won't do today. And what we don't do tomorrow will not be what we'll be doing the day after." By the time architectural copyists had caught on to an idea of Mr. Wright's, he was already on to something new. Mies' credo was just the opposite: "You don't start a new style each Monday."

Mr. Wright felt Mies' warmth and was happy to have his work viewed with understanding. From Racine, we drove to Oak Park to see Unity Temple, a building that illustrates Wright's genius for drawing out the nature of materials with supreme mastery. Built in 1906 in Oak Park, Unity Temple not only expresses the nature of its materials, it is the purest example of Mr. Wright's organic architecture. It is also the only public building of his Oak Park years still standing and is still used for its original function—by descendants of the original clients, the congregation of the Unitarian Universalist Church.

Unity Temple was Mr. Wright's first building in which the nature of the material became one with the basic design concept. The method and materials of construction grow out of the design, from overall massing of the building down to ornament. It was conceived in concrete. It was the first all-concrete building.

Here is the clearest expression of his theories on form and function. The plan and physical form of the structure directly reflect the beliefs of the Unitarian church. Over the entry, the Unitarian statement of purpose is incised into concrete: "For the worship of God and the service of man." Straightforward, unpretentious words. Beliefs that needed a building to match, one without symbolic spires and an image borrowed from the Gothic past.

For "the worship of God," Mr. Wright designed the "temple," one room, square in plan, to serve as the sanctuary. Noble and reserved, the room is at the same time warm and very human. The key to Unitarian worship is the minister's spoken word. To bring the 400 members of the congregation close to their minister, Mr. Wright designed the seating only fifteen rows deep and created three tiers of shallow balconies around the main space, so that no one would be more than forty-five feet away from the speaker. The acoustics are impeccable.

For "the service of man," Mr. Wright designed Unity House, a fellowship hall with kitchen, sewing room, and classrooms, isolated from the sanctuary, yet joined to it by a large, square entrance foyer. Through an entry both joining and separating the two major functions of the church, Mr. Wright integrated the entire structure and achieved a "harmony of the whole."

The site of Unity Temple was far from ideal for a house of worship, even in 1904. Situated at the busy corner of Lake and Kenilworth in Oak Park, the site's main drawback was noise from nearby streetcars and other traffic. Mr. Wright used to tell us, "The trouble with general church design is that you open the door, go into the vestibule and straight into the sanctuary. It cuts the building down the middle, cuts it apart. Part of the genius shown in the design of Unity is the entrance position. Not only does Mr. Wright solve the noise problem by setting the entrance back off the street, but he also leads you most subtly into the

Top: Unity Temple, entrance.

Bottom: Sanctuary end of Unity Temple, showing the pours of concrete. Building across the street is a typical church, with typical center entrance.

71

Entrance inscription, "For the worship of God and the service of man."

building. First you see the building as you approach it, from either street. Then his scheme brings you from the sidewalk up a half-dozen steps onto a platform. From here, he turns you ninety degrees and takes you across the terrace into a low-ceilinged vestibule, where he gives you the option of going either to the sanctuary on one side or the fellowship hall on the other.

When Mr. Wright first discussed this project with Reverend Johonnot and the building committee, he learned the budget was tight—only $45,000. A church in stone would have cost double this amount. As Mr. Wright saw it, there was only one choice for a building material: concrete. Although he describes concrete as the cheapest material, there is no other that could have been used organically to achieve his goal. The beauty of the building is the appearance of one material doing everything— reinforced concrete for walls, roof slab, ornament. In an integrated chorus, subservient materials add their voice: stained glass, lighting fixtures designed in wood, and the wooden organ pipe screens inside.

Poured concrete was a relatively new building material in 1904. Construction workers weren't familiar with it, and apparently they had many problems with Unity. For one thing, they didn't know that the wetter the mix of concrete, the weaker its strength, or that the cantilevered horizontal roof slabs should have had their reinforcing bars above rather than below in the slabs. Since a large expense in concrete is the formwork—wooden "molds" into which the wet concrete is poured to set—Mr. Wright's plan was to reuse the formwork as much as possible to keep construction costs down. Because of this, three sides of Unity are basically identical.

Interior, looking toward the pulpit. Architect designed everything, including electric light fixtures.

Mr. Wright told us a story about the way he achieved the rough texture in the exterior surfaces. Concrete is made of cement, water, and a gravel and sand combination. In constructing Unity, Mr. Wright ordered soap put on the outer wall forms to keep the surface concrete from setting. When the forms were stripped, the walls were scrubbed with brushes to expose the gravel, thus creating a rough surface texture. On closer inspection, the layers of pours could also be seen. Mr. Wright said, "We experimented," meaning himself and Paul Mueller, the builder. Mueller was the one builder with enough vision to take on the project. Most other contractors were afraid of it, and the few bids that came in were well above double the budget. Mueller finished the job in about a year "for a little over the appropriation," as Mr. Wright tells in the *Autobiography*. He'd known Mueller since the early days in Chicago, when Mueller had worked as a construction manager for Adler and Sullivan, and he respected him. Later, he brought Mueller in as builder for Midway Gardens, then took him to Japan for the Imperial Hotel. In 1932, when Mueller visited Taliesin, Mr. Wright showed him great deference as he walked him about the buildings, describing the Fellowship and showing him the drawings of future structures being planned. We apprentices could feel the respect, indebtedness, and strong ties between these two men who had shared experiences. Mr. Wright's interest included the nature of man as well as materials.

When I first saw Unity Temple—on a visit to Oak Park in 1932 with another apprentice—I was impressed by its nobility and solidity. It seemed historic, yet not belonging to a specific period of history. It looked as if it belonged there, as if it meant to stay. On the other hand, it looked smaller than I had expected. I learned later that this is often the case with Wright buildings because Mr. Wright's overall scale was lower. His buildings are in proportion, but they're all proportionately smaller than what our eye is accustomed to today. Even Prairie School architects often maintained the larger scale of Victorian buildings. When Prairie architects copied Mr. Wright's style but not his scale, the buildings seemed awkward, out of human scale.

About 1970, I went out to Oak Park again to have a look at Unity Temple. This time, I'd just returned from a trip to the Netherlands, where elements of Mr. Wright's style were adopted in the 1920's and 1930's. After the Dutch versions, Unity Temple, back in Oak Park, looked pure and pristine and original—until I got a close look. The concrete, porous to begin with, was raw. It had weathered badly. A coat of protective paint applied about ten years earlier hadn't improved it; cracks showed through. Moisture had worked its way in; rust stains appeared where reinforcing bars had been placed too close to the surface; the cornices were cracked. The church knew that repairs had to be made, but couldn't afford them.

Through the generosity of Edgar Kaufmann, whose father was the client for Fallingwater, arrangements were made to restore Unity Temple to its original state. The complex restoration was handled by Mr. Wright's oldest son, Lloyd Wright, working with his son, Eric. By the mid-1970s, they brought the building back to its original texture and color. In 1971, Unity Temple was named a national landmark.

After showing Mies van der Rohe around Oak Park, we went on to the Avery Coonley house in Riverside. This house, completed in 1908, was definitely among the most remarkable of the Prairie houses; it was the most elegant and finely detailed. Given a generous budget, or insisting on one, Mr. Wright bestowed his most loving care on this house, making it a landmark building in his career. We often remarked that his enthusiasm was in direct proportion to the budget. I had visited this estate-sized Prairie house before, with its gardens and pool, its servants' and gardener's quarters. After seeing the very beautiful and delicate ornamental panels in colored tiles that go around the upper story on the exterior, I had wondered what the interior was like. For Mr. Wright, it was no trouble to get into a house. He just rang the bell—when someone answered, he pushed open the door and walked right in.

When he was in Spring Green, talking to the local people, he'd say, "I'm Frank Wright," but to everyone else, it would be, "I'm Frank Lloyd Wright," or "I'm Wright the architect." He had to charm his architectural public, maintain his symbols, but he never put on a big show for the local people. After all, Frank Wright had been among them for years and years, and they'd seen him at every up and down of his life. That day the owners were out, but Mr. Wright introduced himself to the housekeeper and led us in.

After we walked into the Coonley hallway, Mr. Wright showed Mies the two-way-exposure kitchen, which was on the second floor. The ground floor—storage, playrooms—was like a basement raised to the light, since the living spaces were above.

Mr. Wright had known instinctively how to make the Coonley house great. It was all intuition, feeling. The interior, which I now saw for the first time, was classically beautiful. It was amazing how well he handled the composition all the way. The whole, the parts, even down to the stained glass and the murals—it was all absolute perfection. This was the work of an artist totally sure and in control of himself, one of those extraordinary combinations of elements that all fit together to produce a masterpiece. Feeling, emotion, have a great deal to do with producing such a work. So does chemistry between architect and client, how one responds to the other. It's also the combination of creativity and certain feeling at a particular point in an artist's development.

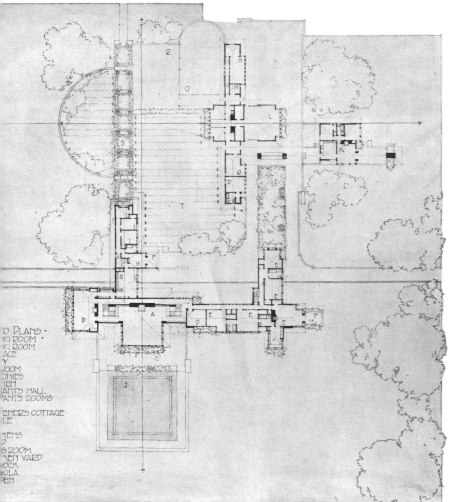

Coonley House, 1908. The young lady is the Coonleys' daughter, now Mrs. Faulkner. Mr. Wright retouched another print of this photograph with his soft pencil to eliminate her—see below.

75

Alterations to Coonley House (compare with picture on p. 75): Mr. Wright added trellises and doors to playroom. *Right:* Addition to master bedroom. Note the wide, flat soffit treatment.

Horse-watering trough at right of entrance. "Foliage" drawn onto photo by Mr. Wright to show growth from pot up to trellis formed out of trim. At right, Mr. Wright's Packard touring car parked in shelter of entryway.

Living room, Coonley House. *Left:* Dining room.
Mr. Wright cut off the lower half of the photographs,
hating furniture that was designed by others.

The Coonley house was designed so that from any window the view was out into the trees. The terrace below was completely screened by rich foliage growing over the trellises. In the dining room near the top of the stairwell, Mr. Wright pointed out the carpet he had designed specially, woven for him in Peking. It took up about half the room. The dining table was placed so that each dinner guest had a view of the outside. We went along the corridor to the living room which, when we saw it in 1937, was almost exactly as it had been originally in 1908, except for the addition of a few more modern pieces of furniture chosen by the owners of that period, who were in the furniture business. Mr. Wright turned on all the living room lights so we could see the continuous mural, showing mostly ferns and birch trees, painted along the inside wall. The entire room, with its calmly abstract carpet also designed by Mr. Wright, was very soft, pastel colors and gold.

We didn't linger long in the Coonley house because Mr. Wright was anxious to have Mies see the Robie house. We made a beeline from Riverside to the south side of Chicago, the section that Mr. Wright boasted he knew so well. He moved up to the front seat, directing where to turn with emphatic certainty. "Turn right here, then turn left." I followed the instructions, but we got lost nonetheless. Finally we drew up to the Robie house, and he had us look at it first from across the street, through the trees. Then we walked across to it, went left and around the end to the entrance. As in other houses, Mr. Wright had designed an unobtrusive, almost hidden entrance. He'd planned the visitor's progression, leading him toward the building, making him turn, bringing him around to the front door, then making him change direction once more, a whole architectural sequence, one event after another.

This time for me, more than on any other expedition, I had the feeling of being in the presence of living history. Going through Chicago with Mies, himself an exceptional personality, seeing several Wright houses and knowing that there were dozens more nearby, was an extraordinary experience. There I was, a student of twenty-five, next to the man who had created landmark buildings, who had given a character to an entire city.

We walked into the Robie house unattended. The Chicago Theological Seminary, which had converted it into their quarters, seemed to welcome visitors. As we went around the main floor, Mr. Wright explained to Mies how he had made the space flow completely, with the fireplace being the only interruption between the living and dining areas. Mies didn't ask questions or make any comments, but he kept smiling and nodding his head in understanding. For a man of stolid, Germanic character, Mies was positively radiating. The interpreter, though, was wearing out. We could see Mies sorting out each explanation and filing each experience away in the proper mental drawer.

By the end of that day, there was real friendship and understanding between Mies and Mr. Wright. Philosophically, there was something dear to both men that made a bond between them and didn't need to be spoken. Mies was different from the rest of his colleagues—more soft and human, though his work appears calculated and cold.

Not long after this expedition, Mies was appointed head of the Armour Institute in Chicago, now the Illinois Institute of Technology. Mr. Wright was invited to speak at the inauguration dinner. The evening was interminable and the speeches were successions of platitudes about the greatness of America and the greatness of the country's institutions in general and her architecture in particular. Mr. Wright, never one to abide empty flattery or listen patiently to anyone else's lectures, walked up to the microphone when he was called at last to introduce

Mies. He looked at the audience, said simply, "I give you Mies," and strode off.

Mr. Wright enjoyed shopping and delighted in terrorizing store personnel. Always trying to bargain. Luxuries came first, then necessities—a lifelong trait. He loved acting out his own myth in public, and I knew well enough, from all the times before, that each time I went shopping with him he would cause a scene. Belligerent—yes, but funny too. With or without an audience. The show he put on was not only for the benefit of his public. That was the way he was. This time we went to Marshal Field's department store. In an extravagant mood, Mr. Wright announced he would buy a hat for Mrs. Wright. What she needed was a new hat. He examined every hat, twirling each one on the end of his cane and parading it in the air in front of us. "Well, Edgar," he asked, "how do you think Mrs. Wright would look in this?" He especially liked one decorated with cherries. It reminded him of what his mother once wore. He ended up with five very expensive models. Summoning the buyer, he motioned with his cane to the stack of hats on the table and demanded, "How much will you take for the lot?" And he got a discount.

He always knew how to command a reduction. Even so, I thought five hats extravagant at a time when we were skimping at Taliesin, driving on old tires, wearing old clothing, trying to make ends meet.

Our next stop was the book department. The buyer, an older woman, rather quiet and prim, came over and introduced herself. First Mr. Wright asked how his books were doing. Then he inquired in his most guileless manner, "Madam, if you caught a man stealing a Bible, would you call the police?"

On another trip, to Madison, we stopped at a secondhand hardware store owned by Cohen and Levy. He went through the entire shop, picking at the bins, and finally assembled a pile of tools—hammers, saws, wrenches, all used and in fair condition. He said to the shopkeeper, "Add up the cost." The tools came to about $120. "I'll give you $80 for the lot," offered Mr. Wright. But the fellow said, "Nope. That's the price. One-twenty." Mr. Wright shrugged, turned to me, and said, "O. K., Edgar, let's go." As we were walking out, I heard Cohen say something in Yiddish to Levy. When we were outside, Mr. Wright asked if I had understood Cohen's remark. When I translated, "He can lie in hell," Mr. Wright just laughed. You can't win every time.

Certainly the most personal and revealing of Mr. Wright's post-Oak Park buildings is the home he built for himself and Mamah Borthwick Cheney when they returned from Europe in 1911. With the fervor of a man creating a new life for himself,

Edwin H. Chaney house, Oak Park, Illinois, 1904, in a drawing from the Wasmouth edition of Mr. Wright's works. A memorable house to Mr. Wright.

based on a maturely reasoned philosophy, Mr. Wright turned to the Wisconsin country, where his mother's clan had its roots, and began to build "Taliesin." Away from the gossip of a conservative suburb, Mr. Wright looked forward to a quiet, full life with his companion, whom he no doubt wanted to marry. Neither he nor she, however, could obtain a divorce. Work continued, for he still had a few clients who understood his point of view and did not judge his architecture by scrutinizing his private life.

Apart from the important but relatively few residential designs that filled the years from 1911 to 1914, one of Mr. Wright's most significant commissions was an entertainment restaurant in downtown Chicago, the Midway Gardens. A symbol of the high-spirited years just preceding the bleak decades of war and the Depression, Midway Gardens was conceived as a grand-scale European café. Complete with a complex of outdoor terraces for dining and sophisticated musical entertainment, it also offered a "winter garden" for indoor dining. In spite of money shortage, Midway Gardens was completed in record time and opened for a successful first season. But by the second year, World War I had broken out; currents changed, internal management problems came up, and the Gardens were eventually sold to a brewery, which cheapened it with beer-garden decoration and taste. Finally, with the advent of prohibition, the Gardens became anachronistic and were closed before they could deteriorate further. When they were torn down to make way for an "auto laundry," Mr. Wright took special pleasure in knowing that the demolition company went bankrupt in the work because the structure was so strong. Years later, on a trip to Chicago, I visited the old site and, picking through the rubble, came across a few of the magnificent, semiabstract sculpted heads. I dug them out to bring back to Taliesin.

In Midway Gardens, not only did Mr. Wright create an extraordinary architectural composition, but he overlaid the entire complex with intricate and original ornament. Sculpture everywhere, mostly in the form of stylized human figures. Sculpture conceived spontaneously in Mr. Wright's imagination, in which historians have found reminiscences of Mayan or Indian art and forecasts of Europe's art of the late 1920s and 1930s.

While construction of Midway Gardens was still going on, in 1914, Mr. Wright was having lunch with his son John on the site when he received word of an unbelievable tragedy at Taliesin: A servant, gone mad, had killed seven people including Mamah Borthwick Cheney and her two visiting children, and had set fire to the buildings.

In the nine years I lived and worked with Mr. Wright he never mentioned the name of this extraordinary woman. And I never had the courage to ask about her. I suspect he might have wanted to talk, if I had known how to phrase the questions, but he kept the memory of her far within his own thoughts.

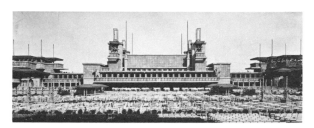

Midway Gardens, Chicago, Illinois, 1913.

5

When biographers discuss Mr. Wright, they refer to the time from the 1890s to about 1910 as "the Oak Park period." While most of Mr. Wright's work in that time was done in and around Chicago, he also designed a number of important buildings outside Chicago. There were, for example, the houses for Thomas Hardy on Lake Michigan in Racine, Wisconsin, the Boynton house in Rochester, New York, and the Francis W. Little house in Wayzata, Minnesota, completed in 1914. This last house was carefully dismantled. Its living room was reconstructed in the American Wing of the Metropolitan Museum in New York, and its library can be seen in the Allentown Art Museum in Pennsylvania.

One of the most innovative designs of this period was the Larkin Building in Buffalo, 1904. The Larkin Company, which began as the Larkin Soap Company and later became a mail-order and wholesale firm, was established by John Larkin and Elbert Hubbard. Socially concerned, they believed that a customer who bought a product of the company should also buy into the company's profit sharing. So, with every bar of soap, the customer also got a minute share in the Larkin Company. The more soap the public bought, the less stock the company owned in itself. The curious thing about the company—aside from its peculiar economics and the tight, rather complicated interweaving of family relationships—is that the top administrative staff all became Mr. Wright's clients. Elbert Hubbard was by far the most picturesque of the group. His philosophy and ambitions were well known, and though his notions did not bring in great profits for the Larkin Soap Company, his name was popularized through the Arts and Crafts movement as the American folk equivalent of England's William Morris. In 1893 he sold his partnership in the Larkin Company and became the central figure of the Roycrofter artists' community in East Aurora, near Buffalo. Inspired by the ideals of Morris, he set up a printing press to publish his own writing, then a bindery, then a leathercraft shop. After the turn of the century he began producing handcrafted furniture of a simple and austere design, which was used to furnish the Roycrofter guest inn and was sold to the public as well. Elbert Hubbard's end was as intriguing as his life: he and his wife, Alice, disappeared on the *Lusitania* in 1915.

John Larkin, chief administrator of the Larkin Company, was married to one of Hubbard's sisters. When Hubbard retired from the company his position was taken over by Darwin D. Martin. It was D. D. Martin's brother in Chicago, W. E. Martin, who knew Frank Lloyd Wright and sparked the meeting that led to six Buffalo commissions. The Martin brothers were co-owners of the E-Z Stove Polish Company in Chicago, for which Mr. Wright designed a factory in 1905. According to one story, Darwin Martin had visited his brother's new Wright house in Oak Park in 1903. He was so impressed that he decided to see the Wright studio. According to another story, the Martin brothers were driving through Chicago when they saw a Wright house; they were so taken by it that each commissioned Mr. Wright to design a house. That's the version Mr. Wright used to tell, and it bears the imprint of his customary romanticizing. In any case, Darwin Martin asked Mr. Wright to see his property in Buffalo, on Jewett Parkway, where he planned to build two houses. The first was to be a home for Martin's sister, Mrs. George Barton, and her family. Mr. Wright began this house in 1903. The Martin house, started in the following year, was on a much grander scale, physically and financially. Martin had imposed no budget, so Mr. Wright was completely free to express the total building and all its details and furnishings in the most elaborate way. All in all, the costs, it is said, came to $300,000—in 1904! Martin introduced the Larkin Company to Mr. Wright, and the Larkin Administration Building was soon under way.

Mr. Wright later designed a house for the company's advertising manager, Alexander Davidson—a "budget house," you could tell, for it was done in stucco. Years later, around 1927, when Mr. Wright designed a country house for the Martins, Davidson asked him to create a system of prefabricated farm buildings. These were never actually constructed, but we at

Alexander Davidson house, Buffalo, New York.

Top: Larkin Administration Building, Buffalo, New York, 1903. Exterior showing articulated stair towers at corners.

Bottom: Central open interior court and skylight of general office area.

Taliesin worked on the model for them, which was later exhibited along with the Broadacre City model. Mr. Wright also designed a house for the Larkin Company attorney, W. R. Heath, who was married to another of Elbert Hubbard's sisters. The plot continued into the next generation, when Heath's minister son Paul engaged me to design a budget Presbyterian church.

The Larkin Building, in downtown Buffalo, was monumental and imposing. It had the character of a massive concrete structured building, rather than a brick-faced one, which it really was, and it incorporated a number of architectural innovations. Technically, it was the first air-conditioned and one of the first fireproofed buildings, but its most remarkable feature is the use of interior space in a way that combines stately dignity with the naturalness of the human scale. (It was torn down in 1950, for economic reasons.) Just as Mr. Wright wanted to change people's lives by the kind of houses and furnishings he created for them, so he also wanted to improve the lives of working people. For the Larkin Company, he designed the first steel office furniture—desks, chairs, and all the accessories.

The Larkin Building, like the Johnson Building thirty years later, was a total integration of form and function, of location, materials, and furnishings. Each was an organic, complete continuity unto itself. The common bond between these two administrative buildings is that both were commissioned by progressive-thinking businessmen who ran progressive firms, who had great concern for their employees, and who genuinely humanized their companies. It was only natural that these men looked on Mr. Wright—with his boldly expressed concepts and high ideals—as the *interpreter* of their ideas. He gave physical reality to their philosophies. And each of these commissions gave rise to a series of other buildings. Johnson, for example, had dismissed his first architect because the man had no feeling for the idea behind the building. But Mr. Wright caught the inspiration. Mr. Larkin and Mr. Johnson could look at their buildings and see *themselves.* They saw a handsome structure and a real one, embodying human feelings and ideals—which is what makes architecture, at this level, a personal experience. Mr. Wright wanted architecture to be a human experience, ever changing, ever new, ever responsive. He knew far too well that the moment individualistic architecture is stuffed into the framework of an establishment bureaucracy, its growth is cut off.

In the Taliesin Fellowship, we came to expect the unexpected. One spring day three of us apprentices were to make a trip to Pittsburgh, but—found ourselves standing in front of the Larkin Building in Buffalo.

That May morning Mr. Wright, in city clothes, came over

to my table and announced, "We're leaving for Pittsburgh in half an hour. Get Manuel—tell him to bring his tools—and Bob Mosher." He was all ready to leave, but this was the first I'd heard of it. We were used to short-notice expeditions, never knowing if we'd be gone for the afternoon or for weeks. This time, we were going to Bear Run, not far from Pittsburgh, where the Kaufmanns' house, Fallingwater, was under construction. I rounded up Manuel, who would stay in Pittsburgh, constructing Mr. Kaufmann's private office, and Bob, who was going to work at the Bear Run site. It was exciting to go out into the field, where a building was emerging from the plans we had worked on.

Manuel, a Nicaraguan with a hairline moustache, was a superb woodworking craftsman. He had come to Taliesin, he thought, to study architecture. Once his real talents were known, however, Mr. Wright never let him out of the woodworking shop. Manuel's reverence for Mr. Wright was such that he made an elegant velvet-lined box to store a pencil given to him by Mr. Wright.

I ran to the kitchen to find Bob, who hadn't been able to avoid kitchen duty. There he was, scraping vegetables. "Hey, Bob!" I said, trying to keep my voice down, "Mr. Wright says we're going to Pittsburgh right away. Be sure to take enough clothing—you're going to stay at Bear Run!" He put down the pan and said calmly to the cook, "Mabel, may I go to the toilet?" We both knew that if she found out he was leaving, there'd be nothing but delays and complications. We left the kitchen nonchalantly, then bolted to our rooms, laughing as we put our clothes and equipment together for the trip.

The three of us joined Mr. Wright in the red Ford convertible, piled Manuel's tools in the trunk and drove off toward Chicago. As soon as we were in the car, Mr. Wright called out, "Let's tap the cesspool!" That meant the radio. As we rode, he kept his cane next to him on the front seat, tapping it against his foot as he talked.

Instead of going straight across to Pittsburgh, as anyone else would have done, Mr. Wright had us drive to Indiana first, so we could visit his architect son John. We all walked the dunes at that end of Lake Michigan. Then we meandered up to Detroit and crossed over into Canada. No special reason. If we expected one thing, he did another. If we did something one way on one day, it was not necessary to do it the same way the next. Coming back from Canada, we went through Niagara Falls. When we got to the border, the customs man asked, "All of you born in the United States?" Before we could stop him, Manuel yelled out, "Born in Nee-kah-RAAH-wah" and then admitted he hadn't brought his papers. None of us knew we were going through Canada, so it had never occurred to Manuel to bring his documents. "Follow me," said the official, and we watched him

Above: Mr. Wright had us stop to pay homage to Louis Sullivan's Prudential Building in Buffalo.

Below: Sullivan's only New York City building, on Bleecker Street.

lead Manuel off to the customs detention office. That was it for Mr. Wright. He got furious, burst out of the car, and besieged the office. I waited in the car for a while, then got curious. I went to the office to see what was up. There was Mr. Wright stomping around and declaring to everyone that he was a great American, that he was a friend of Carl Sandburg and Clarence Darrow, that he was an internationally known architect, that he'd never do anything that wasn't thoroughly American. The customs officials were completely dismayed. They let Manuel go, and we returned to the car and drove on toward Buffalo. Within five minutes, Mr. Wright was snoozing. He could fall asleep anywhere, anytime.

We hadn't known until we got to Chicago that we were going to stop in Buffalo. But we suspected some deviation from the direct route, since by this time we were well aware that the shortest road between two points was by way of a Wright building. Or two or three. Mr. Wright probably hadn't been in Buffalo for years—perhaps he stopped there briefly around 1926, when he designed the country house for the Martins, but he hadn't really spent time there since doing the Larkin Building. This trip was an opportunity for him to show us his "children" and Louis Sullivan's Prudential Building.

Our first visit was to the Larkin Building—unannounced, naturally. As we walked in, Mr. Wright described the air-conditioning system he had devised: air blown over ice to cool it, then circulated through the rest of the building. It was also here that Mr. Wright first used one of his favorite inventions—the wall-hung toilet, along with ceiling-hung stall partitions. He was so proud of this that he charged into the nearest rest rooms to show us. It happened to be the ladies room and it was quite busy. Ignoring the astonished ladies, Mr. Wright went directly to the closest ceiling-hung stall, swung open the door with his cane, and exclaimed, "There it is! The first wall-hung water closet!"

The executive offices of the Larkin Company had been moved across the street. After our tour of the original building, Mr. Wright crossed to the other building and announced to the receptionist that he wanted to see the Larkins. A son of Mr. Wright's 1903 client was president at the time, and other members of the family were still in the company. We were asked to lunch in the executive dining room, where perhaps fifteen of us, altogether, met around one big table. A most cordial reception.

Lunch was simple: an enormous amount of asparagus with hollandaise sauce and salad. One of the Larkins explained, "We like to take advantage of the food that's in season. Can't get enough of it." It was obviously the season for asparagus. Mr. Wright agreed with him; he too liked to eat whatever fruit or vegetable was in season. That's being organic. What came out in the garden, that's what went on the table. Whenever he ate raspberries or blackberries or huckleberries, he'd say with a twinkle, "God might have made a better berry than the strawberry—but he never did."

We finished our lunch and relaxed into conversation. Mr. Wright told the Larkins a story about their father, the founder, who had asked him to design a great building. Mr. Wright said that after working on the design for some time, he'd decided to pull the stair towers out of the building center and place them in outside corners, in a strongly articulated way. Larkin senior asked whether this would be more costly. Mr. Wright answered, "I don't think it would be more than an additional $26,000." "All right, then. Build it like that, with the extra $26,000," said Mr. Larkin. Mr. Wright went on to praise Mr. Larkin's understanding and foresight, his appreciation of new architectural ideas. "Mr. Wright," interrupted one of the Larkins, "your story is true as far as you went. But according to Dad, when the building was completed, the additional cost wasn't $26,000, it was $62,000." A great quiet ensued.

After lunch, the Larkins arranged for us to visit the Darwin D. Martin house, which Mr. Wright had begun designing in 1904 for the company's co-director. In his usual style, Mr. Wright rang the bell and walked in, ignoring the caretakers. D. D. Martin had died earlier that year and the family was no longer living in the house, but it was in mint condition. We went through the ground floor and followed Mr. Wright upstairs. Facing us, at the head of the stairs, was a grandfather clock designed by Mr. Wright. On the left was a portrait of Mrs. Martin in what might have been a Frank Lloyd Wright frame.

D. D. Martin house, Buffalo, New York, 1904—grandfather's clock at top of stairs.

Martin house "tree-of-life" bedroom casement windows—Mr. Wright's description. A museum recently purchased one for $7500.

We admired the stained glass with its tree-of-life pattern. Most of the rooms, except the master bedroom, were unfurnished. We went down to the basement because Mr. Wright wanted to show us the system of construction he had used for the house—steel beams and poured concrete. The house had no wine cellar, as Mr. Wright explained to us, because the Martins were teetotaling Christian Scientists, and he couldn't resist one of his favorite quips: "They're neither Christians nor scientists." The low walls in front of the house were crumbling from moisture that had worked its way in. We walked around and through the gallery to the greenhouse or conservatory. The caretaker told us the family hadn't used it for several years because the pipes of the central steam system had rusted in the concrete and leaked.

In going through the house we tried out the great "barrel chairs" Mr. Wright had designed for the living room. Not long after this tour, when we started work on the Johnson house, I asked Mr. Wright if the barrel chairs could be made again. They were extremely handsome. He recalled that the first ones, of heavy oak, had been made by the Matthews woodworking company in Milwaukee. He always remembered details—names and places. We found the company, under a new name, and learned that they still had the original full-scale drawings of the chair. Then he redesigned it.

Just like Mr. Wright. He couldn't leave anything alone. A detail that had been settled perfectly one day would be changed the next. He changed the wood of the barrel chair, changed the slats, changed the proportions, and made two versions—large and small. He ordered some in oak for the Johnson house and some

Side and back views of "barrel chair" and small pull-up chair; flower stands.

Living room–dining room, some eighty feet long, typical cove lighting.

Below: Originally a reception room, with bronze firewood boxes.

Right: Edgar Kaufmann viewing pull-up chairs, questioning their origin—either Wright or Roycrofter design.

Stairwell, with added skylight.

House of Martin's sister on same property.

Nearby gardener's cottage, also a Wright design.

in cypress for Taliesin. He loved cypress, called it the "wood eternal." But he had a special affection for swamp cypress, calling it "more eternal." He modified the chairs, making them thinner and more graceful, but they turned out to be less stable.

For every new job—house, office building, church, whatever—Mr. Wright designed new furniture. He didn't think of furniture, as individual pieces, but as parts of a whole. We used to compare his method of furniture design with the approach of the Internationalists. Mies and Breuer designed *one* chair and used it forever, in any setting. They merchandised everything. To Mr. Wright, chairs were a sort of demon. He deplored the "stuffed-box-for-sitting-in" as he lamented the boxed-in "box-for-living-in." For some reason, he considered the seated posture of the human body particularly inelegant and said, "The only attractive posture of relaxation is that of reclining." Nonetheless, his clients needed chairs. His discomfort about the necessity of chairs is reflected in the chairs themselves. They're not comfortable. And though he always tried to design chairs in harmony with a particular building, most of his chairs were heavy, clumsy, and angular. Even he complained, "All my life I've been black-and-blue bumping into my own furniture."

The Martin house is interesting in that it had two front doors, one leading to the reception hall and one almost directly off the *porte-cochère,* an early-day carport where carriages or autos were parked. It is the only opulent Wright house prior to his own Taliesin, built in 1911, that didn't get a watering trough by the front entrance. Client Martin was the modern man—his horse-and-buggy days were over by 1905. Mr. Wright claimed that the house was on the wrong side of the tracks, but Mr. Martin wanted a house surrounded by lots of land. Even if he didn't live in the fashionable part of town, Mr. Martin could easily drive to work in his automobile. The automobile was his outreach.

The Martin house floor plan designated a room near one of the entrances as "bursar." Mr. Martin conducted some business at home, and this was his home office. There was a separate, second living room between the bursar's room and the other main entrance. Coming through the formal front door, we entered a two-story foyer and saw a long hallway, with stained glass windows on both sides all the way down to the greenhouse. One of Mr. Wright's favorite statues stood at the end—a plaster reproduction of the Greek winged victory. This was the only piece of Western sculpture he tolerated, and he placed copies in many of his buildings.

In the drafting room at Taliesin, Mr. Wright had a large plan of the Martin house pinned up on the door to the photography closet. He admired this plan as a beautiful abstraction. Not only did he expect a drawing to be technically perfect, but he wanted it to be a work of art. I passed that drawing hundreds of times in the years I spent at Taliesin and must have absorbed its details subliminally.

The Martin house is a good example of how Mr. Wright chose the "grammar" for a building and used it consistently down to the smallest details. He insisted that to create a house that is a work of art, the architect, as artist, needs to express a "consistent thought-language in his design." By grammar, he meant: the relationship of the elements to the whole, governed by a regulating system. For the Martin house, Mr. Wright used one kind of brick outside, so he used the same brick on the inside—with gold leaf in all horizontal joints between the bricks, so that the material seemed to shimmer. In keeping with the grammar, the tile on the floor of the exterior porch was the same as the tile on the floor inside. He used only one kind of plaster—sand-floated with integral color. And only one kind of wood: oak. The chairs and tables were oak and so was all the wood trim. The total feeling of the house was of one stripe, from the overall plan down to the furniture, the door jambs, and the window frames.

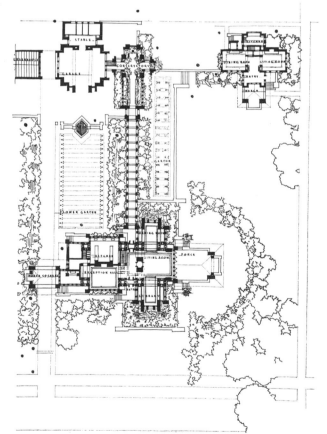

Plan of Martin property, sister's house at upper right.

In 1936, D. D. Martin died. His son, D. R. Martin, considered donating the house either to the city or to the University of Buffalo as a branch library. His offer was rejected, and the Martin house slipped into a dark period. Upkeep and taxes became increasingly burdensome, so that in 1946 the city took over the property in a tax-foreclosure sale (for $74,468 in back taxes and a cash payment of $394.53). The house deteriorated silently. In 1951 the Catholic Diocese of Buffalo bought the property, planning to make it into summer quarters for the first community of Piarist Fathers in this country. This project didn't work out, and the house remained untenanted. It had already stood empty for twelve years. At one point it even seemed the house might be lost to the demolition men or to real estate exploitation, but in 1953 a local architect who liked the house bought it for himself. Sebastian Toriello set up his office in the basement and designed a new office entrance through the garden. He divided the rest of the house into three separate apartments, but unfortunately these did not relate to the original plan of the rooms. There were two apartments in the back, one upstairs and one downstairs, and his own apartment, part of the upper story plus the living room, dining room, and kitchen. To raise money for repairs and restoration, Toriello sold half of the two-acre site to developers, who built three two-story apartment buildings on their half. Much of the effect of Martin house was lost when its conservatory and gallery, the stables, and the garage were demolished to make way for the new apartment buildings. The proposed apartments were not put up without protest. The community challenged the city planning commission's approval of the project, but after hearings the commission's decision held. This often happens.

Again, in 1966, the Martin house was offered for sale, and this time its fate was more fortunate. Martin Meyerson, who was president of the State University of New York at Buffalo, knew of the house, its predicament and its historical importance. He and his wife persuaded the university to buy it, as a home for the president. At $60,000, it cost the university only about $5.00 a square foot. The house would again become a one-family dwelling; after the restoration, it would serve a dual function, as official residence and as entertainment focus for the university.

At this point, because my long association with Mr. Wright and my interest in the house were well known, the head of the State University Construction Fund telephoned to ask if I would take charge of revitalizing the Martin house. The query was put simply, almost in a casual way. I was electrified. I was moved by memories of the Buffalo-Pittsburgh expedition on which Mr. Wright introduced us to the house.

My first step was to make some minor but necessary alterations—to install a modern kitchen and put a good-sized skylight over the dark stairs. Mrs. Martin had always complained that the

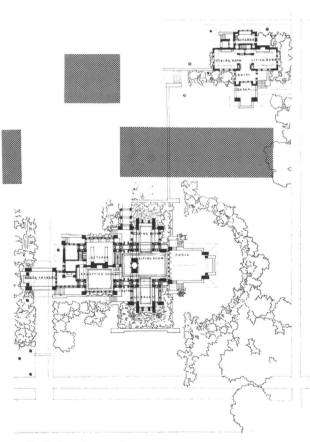

Dark tinted areas show present two-story apartment house on Martin site.

house was too dark. Mr. Wright had tried to lighten it, unsuccessfully, by adding several small skylights. The colors throughout the house were also dark. The woodwork was dark oak and the floors dark brown. The original effect—which included dark brocaded upholstery—had been lightened by soft Japanese prints hung everywhere. Even the great living room seemed dark because of the large porch that blocked out the natural light.

When the State University bought the house, a suggested renovation was to close in the porch. I mentioned this to Mr. Wright's older architect son, Lloyd, who said vehemently, "They ought to leave that porch the way it is. Dad never intended for it to be closed in." Which was true. Lloyd's words reminded me of the drafting room at Taliesin. When Mr. Wright wasn't sure whether he wanted to change a detail, he'd stew for a minute and storm out saying, "Leave it alone!"

We made many repairs on the Martin house, but there were some major, very costly ones that we could not undertake. The roof structure, for example, is in need of repair. Its broad overhangs are sagging and seem to mock the sharpness of Mr. Wright's original Prairie house lines. As to the interior, we kept the Wright character by using his typical earth colors, in lighter tones, even in the furniture. Some of the original furniture designed by Wright was tracked down—the grandfather clock at the top of the stairs, two barrel chairs, and several flower stands. We also used ten chairs and a side table that had once been in the nearby Heath house, found in New England, bronze fireplace wood boxes by Wright, and some of his sofas and armchairs, possibly Roycrofter made.

More than twenty years after Mr. Wright completed Martins' house, they asked him to design a summer house in the town of Derby, twenty miles west of Buffalo. He didn't supervise the construction of this house, "Graycliff." When we finished our tour of the buildings in Buffalo, Mr. Wright decided to drive out and visit "Graycliff." The Martin family had moved to Derby, but they were away. The caretaker let us in. All the furniture was covered with sheets for protection. Mr. Wright led us in, surveyed the main floor, and directed us to take off the covers. He began to rearrange the furniture—beginning, as was his way, with the piano. Next he instructed us to get knives from the kitchen and to cut huge bunches of spring flowers and branches outside in the garden. We filled all the living room vases and pots. (I remember it was spring because we had asparagus for lunch.) Mr. Wright left a note for the Martins, something like this: "Stopped by to visit you. FLLW, your Architect." And again we were off.

On the way down to Pittsburgh, we spent the night in a hotel. We had dinner in the hotel's would-be elegant restaurant. On the way in, Mr. Wright snapped a flower out of a table centerpiece and stuck it in his lapel.

The first apprentices in the Taliesin drafting room got to know the Imperial Hotel, Tokyo, intimately, line by line. In the first winter of the Fellowship, as an exercise in drawing and making plates, we drew up rooms—plans and furniture—from the hotel. It was Wisconsin winter weather, cold and bitter. The apprentices were divided up into "ins" and "outs." One group went to the woods Mondays, Wednesdays, and Fridays to cut wood for the boilers; the other group went on alternate days. Those who stayed back stoked the boilers and worked in the drafting room on drawings of earlier Wright projects.

Many of us disliked the plan of the Imperial because it seemed so traditional, with classic H-shape and strong axis and sub-axis. Henry Klumb, senior apprentice in charge of the drafting room, said, "Some day that building will be gone and all that'll be left will be Mr. Wright's drawings." And Henry's words came true in 1968. While we were drawing, Mr. Wright would come by; he'd stop at each apprentice's table and pencil in some lines. He'd tell stories of the Imperial as he drew in the details. He'd describe the carpets he designed and the built-in furniture, the little trapdoor he made from each guest room to the corridor, so a valet could take the shoes at night to have them polished—so the shoes wouldn't clutter up the hallways. He told unbelievable stories about the construction. Each time the workmen were paid, they would desert the job until their money ran out, which gave them about four days off each week. The Japanese system of building seemed to involve as many bribes and kickbacks as our own. They stuck to their own methods when it came to construction techniques, and no amount of screaming and stamping by foreman Paul Mueller could make them change their ways. They refused to use the heavy Western scaffolding, insisting that their flimsy laced bamboo framework was better.

Beyond question, the Imperial Hotel was a monumental example of the Wright genius. To create a total environment, he engaged himself to the fullest in the building's design and construction, from the purchase of a stone quarry to the delineation of chinaware for the dining room. Mr. Wright *became* the Imperial Hotel, and it consumed more and more of him during the nine years of its realization. By the time he left Japan in 1922, on his last trans-Pacific trip, he was exhausted, physically run down to the point of being ill, depressed, and wearied by the petty machinations of gigantic proportions that had underlain the entire project. His moral fatigue and the whole intricate story of the hotel have caused many of us to wonder whether any architect should be entrusted with comprehensive design responsibility over every detail, at every level of the building, and whether an architect should commit himself so completely to one commission. But, then, who has the right to bridle genius?

Imperial Hotel, Tokyo, 1919, soon after completion. Rickshas were still in use.

This great hotel, the Imperial, the source of much unhappiness, has been called "the victim of Wright's own perfectionism." Louis Sullivan wrote in 1923 that the building was "a great gift to endure for generations of all time," and yet the hotel lived only forty-five years. The Imperial outlived its justification, twice escaping demolition, and from its very beginnings brought into question its own usefulness, weighed against the effort and expense that created it and financially destroyed its backers. The initial budget stipulated two million yen; the final expense was nine or nine-and-a-half million yen, or about $4.75 million. Construction time was triple the original estimated, and before the end—with the board and its backers foundering in quarrels, short money, gangsterism, and petty intrigue—Mr. Wright left Japan forever. Building "organically" in the United States was tough enough, but in Japan of the early twentieth century—still characterized by feudal methods and attitudes—imagine the difficulties.

How did Frank Lloyd Wright, architect of the American Midwest and creator of the Prairie house, come to Japan to build a hotel for the Mikado's visiting dignitaries? There are two versions to the story, as usual: his "official" one (in the *Autobiography*) and the other.

After the days of Commodore Perry, when Japan began opening up to the West in the mid-nineteenth century, the Emperor commissioned a grand hotel to house Western-style diplomatic functions and important visitors who were not accustomed to kneeling, sitting, sleeping, and generally living on the floor, in Japanese fashion. The first Imperial was designed and built by Japanese firms; construction was supervised by a German office. A number of prominent Japanese businessmen, together with the Imperial Household, raised the necessary capital and obtained rights (from the Ministry of Foreign Affairs) to a large site in central Tokyo. The design of the first Imperial was decidedly European, with French roofs and classical ornament; it had only sixty guest rooms. By 1910 this hotel was outdated. Overly grand in style, dank and dark to begin with, it had acquired with age an additional characteristic—mold, whose odor throughout the building was inescapable. And it was too small. Increasing numbers of visitors were arriving from the West.

For the next hotel venture, the Emperor's entourage again enlisted Japan's leading capitalists and a commission was dispatched worldwide, so the story goes, to find a suitable architect for the new Imperial Hotel. It is at this point that Mr. Wright's romantic and automatic legend-making mechanism comes into play. He said in his autobiography that a Japanese commission had traveled worldwide seeking an architect. They became interested in Wright's houses of the Middle West, which they thought would look well in Japan. So they sought out Mr. Wright at Taliesin. The commission, including the Imperial Hotel manager, Hayashi, and Yoshitaki, the architect, did indeed come to Taliesin for a week in 1915. However, their trip was little more than a formality, since it already seemed quite definite that Mr. Wright was their architect. They may have come simply as diplomatic envoys to have a look at his work.

The *Autobiography* neglects to say that in the spring of 1913 Mr. Wright made an unpublicized trip to Japan with Mamah Borthwick Cheney. Although this trip is never mentioned in his books or articles, it has been verified through journalistic sources, and it is known that he traveled at the invitation of the Emperor. It presumably came about through contacts he had made earlier, on his 1905 trip to Japan with clients and his first wife. On that visit, he met the noted architect and professor Takeda, who presented him with fifteen woodblock prints, the beginning of a superb collection. Mr. Wright became an authority on Japanese prints; some of the ones he owned can be seen in the great Spaulding collection in Boston. Takeda, who was enthusiastic about Mr. Wright's work, may have helped him secure the commission for the Imperial. The business manager of the old hotel, Aisaku Hayashi, was another principal in the Imperial

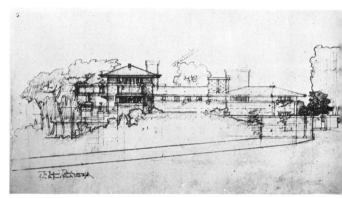

Inscription: "To Professor Takeda from his friend Frank Lloyd Wright."

Design for Odawara Hotel in Nagoya Japan, 1912, not executed.

School of the Free Spirit, completed after Mr. Wright left Japan.

drama. He had traveled extensively as representative of an important Japanese art dealer and was familiar with principal Western cities, both European and American, as well as new directions in art and architecture. He may even have met Mr. Wright during his travels. As for the "commission" that had gone "round the world" to search for an architect, Hayashi's travels as an art dealer may have been the basis for the romanticized version.

When Mr. Wright visited in Japan in 1913, he apparently received the contract to design the hotel from approved preliminary plans. When he returned to Taliesin in Wisconsin, he set about converting the plans into working drawings. He was forced to put this work aside temporarily a year later when Midway Gardens required all his attention. His career was an architectural juggling act—one crisis job after another.

Aside from an intense desire to escape Taliesin after the tragic fire of 1914, and a general desire to leave the United States for a time and see new lands, Mr. Wright had other reasons for going to Tokyo. He must have thought the Imperial Hotel would establish him as the world's most highly reputed architect. By 1913, in his mid-forties, he had outgrown Oak Park and the Midwest, lost his taste for smaller work, and was looking for new horizons. He was aware that every diplomat and dignitary who visited Japan would stay at the Imperial Hotel and that the architect's name would be remembered by all. Later, he even designed stationery with this colophon: Frank Lloyd Wright, Incorporated—Chicago, New York, Los Angeles, Tokyo. Japan was his new frontier, free of the centuries-old traditions of Europe which he found so odious and false.

From his first encounter with the Japanese print, he was enamored of Japan's art and philosophical approach to beauty— close to his own ideals. In a published essay, "The Japanese Print," he presents his theories of aesthetics succinctly and directly. He speaks not as a man who designs buildings but as an artist and poet. He could be a businessman, and he knew how to run a farm, and he was involved with many other interests—but he saw the world with an artist's eye. Beauty and harmony were the qualities he sought in everything—a face, a woman's dress, an arrangement of greens, an Oriental sculpted figure, a house on its site, a landscape. His extraordinarily retentive mind stored visual details, but it was not the mind of a cataloguer. He bought art objects because they were beautiful, not for documentary reasons.

In placing his favorite objects around Taliesin, Mr. Wright was always composing still-lifes of Buddha figures and Oriental bowls. Even in his office there were samples of bricks and other building materials, memorabilia, fragments of buildings he had done, out of which he made compositions. Nothing was haphazard, nothing was left frozen in a conservative symmetry.

Oriental objects at Taliesin, obtained in Japan by Mr. Wright. It is said that he spent his entire fee from the Imperial Hotel—some $300,000—on Oriental art. The collection, which arrived in Spring Green by train, was a full carload.

Stone Buddha used as terminal for wall.

Cast-iron Buddha. Mr. Wright changed location of his artwork, for different orientation, as the spirit moved him.

His concern for art in his clients' homes was just as serious. In one client's house, he rearranged all the objects on a ledge. That client, sensitive to Mr. Wright's judgment, carefully marked the spot of each piece, so that it could be replaced exactly after cleaning. Mr. Wright always tried to instill this appreciation of beauty and harmonious arrangement in apprentices and clients.

Beauty, to Mr. Wright, was not a matter of taste. It was neither relative nor subject to the fluctuations of history or culture. Beauty was everlasting, an absolute quality existing in a "realm of essences." Only the object or characteristic that reflected these essences could be called beautiful. Mr. Wright's concept reflected the platonic belief in the eternal idea, centered around the acknowledgment of universal principles, perfect forms, preexisting and unchanging essences of all things, material and abstract. For the architect, perfection of form is expressed through geometry—the principle of form. Thus, Mr. Wright said, the form in any design is its structure, the organization of its parts into a unified and vital totality.

In Japanese art, Mr. Wright recognized ideals akin to his own. He had an intuitive understanding of Japanese aesthetics. He emphasized the Japanese artist's sensitivity to the geometry of form, to geometry as the subject's aesthetic skeleton, as the "suggestive soul" of the artist's work.

What this means, in terms of art or architecture or any other aesthetic approach, is cutting away excess, stripping the flesh, the fat, the muscle, even the bone, and peeling away the layers of materiality down to the very spirit.

By the time he became familiar with Japanese prints, as a young man, Mr. Wright was already conscious of this necessary "elimination of the insignificant, process of simplification." The prints intensified his awareness of it. In the Fellowship later, we saw that this was not his approach to architecture alone; it was how he interpreted and absorbed all that he came in touch with, trying to simplify and reduce everything to basic terms, whether in architecture, cooking, or government.

Mr. Wright often told us of his distaste for the Renaissance and indeed for all European art that followed. He felt that Japanese art transcended stylistic devices, personalities, and rigid period distinctions. Japanese prints never lost their magic for him. For apprentices at Taliesin in the early Fellowship years, they came to have a special meaning. At Christmas, there were invariably ten or twelve of us who couldn't get back to our families. Mr. Wright made it a true holiday by giving us each a print. If there were ten of us still at Taliesin, he'd take out fifteen or so prints from the stacks in the vault. We'd draw numbers and choose our prints accordingly, with number one having his pick of the lot. When we had made our selection, Mr. Wright would tell us who each artist was, what the subject was, the history of the print and what series it came from. Somehow there was never a Hokusai—Hiroshigis and actor prints only. He exercised his art critic's judgment on our choices. There were always one or two really fine prints in the batch, and we would see his eyes twinkling as we chose. On the top or across the bottom, he'd write in pencil, "To_____, from FLLW and Olgivanna, 19—." Every so often, he'd take prints he considered too bright (from early impressions) and put them outside in the sun to fade. He could identify the style of every artist and had learned enough Japanese to read the signature. When he came across a print that was somewhat faded—perhaps because it had been turned out at the end of an ink run—he'd touch it up with colored pencils. Like the Japanese, he didn't believe in framing prints. He'd mat the print, stand it up on an easel to be enjoyed for a while, and later change it for another.

Mr. Wright sincerely believed that in the Imperial Hotel he would design a modern building that respected Japanese tradition and fitted in with indigenous architecture. And in this I think he was successful. For its time, the Imperial was "at home" in Japan. For its function, the luxury and grandeur were justified.

Mr. Wright's intention of designing a structure in harmony with its background of Japanese architecture failed to impress everyone. There were those who saw the matter differently, many Japanese among them. From the beginning, they had doubts about the foundations, the structural aspects of the hotel,

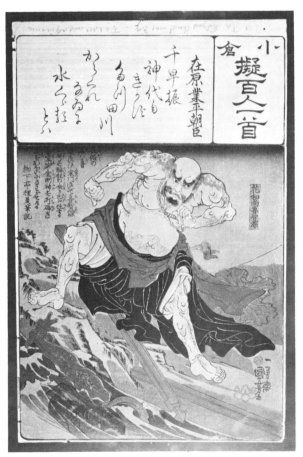

Inscription: "To Edgar, Christmas '34—FLLW and Olgivanna."

101

and its design. They acknowledged its inspired character and found the completed building most beautiful, but never considered it an appropriate companion to their native architecture.

A Czech-born architect, Antonin Raymond, who had met Mr. Wright some years earlier, came to Tokyo early in 1919 as chief draftsman on the site. Mr. Wright used to tell us about Raymond: how he had the airs of a dandy, dressing in the boldest style, putting on his most glittering personality when outside the office. "Now Tony's sporting a boater hat, a cane, and spats!" Mr. Wright would exclaim. The work did not hold Raymond's interest for more than a few months and he began to look around for another job. One day, after working on the Imperial for some time, he came to Mr. Wright and said, "Really, I don't quite know how to tell you this, Mr. Wright, but I've been offered a position with a Japanese firm and they're offering me twice what you're paying me. I just don't know how to handle it." Mr. Wright lost no time in finding a reply. "You've just handled it. You're fired."

Raymond, whom I met in 1967, had a different version of the story: that he was mistreated and underpaid and that Mr. Wright was very difficult.. No one's temper was improved by the difficult living conditions: Mr. Wright, his companion Miriam Noel, his son John, the Raymonds, and Paul Mueller (the foreman imported from Chicago) and his son lived in close quarters in the old Imperial annex.

When Mr. Wright began inspecting the conditions of the site, he found some sixty or seventy feet of soft mud under the surface. It occurred to him that this compressible, cheesy-textured mush could serve as a cushion for the structure. He wondered, "Why not float the building upon it, like a battleship floating on salt water?" Japan was constantly threatened by earthquakes. Their frequency and force reduced the Japanese to terror. Buildings were heaved from their foundations and devastating fires swept through the cities, destroying the paper-and-wood houses by the hundreds.

In his completely original solution to designing an earthquake-proof building, Mr. Wright went against every structural convention of both East and West. Then and now, large Western structures are typically organized over a steel skeleton. This system was used by American construction firms working in Japan at the time of the Imperial project. They set steel frames on long piles driven through sixty or so feet of mud until they hit solid bearing, disregarding the fact that this procedure attached the buildings firmly to the earth. The heavier and more rigid the building, the greater its chance of destruction in a quake, since wave movements of the earth caused the piles to vibrate and thus "rock the structure." The foundations of Wright's Imperial were designed to ride with the earth movement rather than resist it.

This revolutionary and still theoretical foundation design

caused all the trouble for Mr. Wright. The Western Society of American Engineers called the foundation system "unsound." American construction companies in Tokyo, entrenched in conservatism and self-protection, expressed doubt and annoyance over the idea. They were probably angry because Mr. Wright was employing Japanese workmen, but the Japanese were equally angry because the Imperial Hotel was employing a foreign architect. Finally doubt infected even the hotel's Japanese board of directors. Baron Okura was the only member who supported Mr. Wright. With his courageous help—plus the faith of the hotel's general manager Hayashi and the crew of Japanese architecture students—construction was pushed forward. Despite the Baron's encouragement and promise to ensure funds for the outrageously mounting construction costs, few people believed Mr. Wright's design would succeed. The budget had already tripled from the original figure; labor problems were rampant; delays and difficulties in obtaining construction materials were complicated by gangsterism. Mr. Wright's insistence on perfection had not endeared him to the suppliers or workmen. A devastating fire that razed the old Imperial in April 1922 caused enormous financial loss. Finally, Baron Okura, Hayashi, and other Wright partisans resigned from their positions. The fire gave them the pretext to resign. There would be no more money.

Then there was a new catastrophe, an earthquake. Only eleven days after the fire, an earth shock of unusual violence struck Tokyo. Work was going full force on the construction. According to Mr. Wright, it was the worst quake in fifty-two years, the ground swell was tremendous, people were knocked down by the impact, chimneys toppled. The new Imperial Hotel was undamaged! Construction could continue.

Once vindicated, Mr. Wright felt he could leave Japan even though the hotel was not completed. The south wing, which remained to be built, was a repetition of the already finished north wing. He felt that it could be done without his supervision. It was necessary—for economic reasons—to open the hotel before it was completed. On July 1, 1922, the central public space and a handful of guest rooms were inaugurated.

Although Mr. Wright's departure in the fall of 1922 was a grand and emotional farewell, with an unprecedented display of appreciation by the workmen, it had a somber and unsatisfying aspect. Mr. Wright's presence was not welcomed by the new executive officers and, in fact, he was never to see the completed hotel.

The story of the shattering quake that hit Tokyo on September 1, 1923, the day the completed Imperial was scheduled to open, is well known. A radio report listed the Imperial among the buildings destroyed. Mr. Wright waited nearly two anxious weeks to find out what had become of his building. Word

Photograph of Imperial Hotel taken about 1922.

Below: Other views, including one that shows a high-rise building across the street, taken in 1967.

"Peacock" chairs, fireplace, in lobby.
Below: Grand ballroom.

came. The building stood. His colleagues were safe. The building, undamaged by the quake, had provided refuge for disaster victims.

By 1936 preparations had begun for the 1941 Olympics to be held in Japan. There was a serious proposal to demolish the Imperial—which contained only 280 rooms—and replace it with a financially more realistic structure. Protest was strong even though the Imperial was by this time no more practical financially than a three-story motel in New York's Times Square. The hotel was reprieved by World War II. Near the end of the war, an American incendiary bomb hit the ballroom by mistake, but most of the hotel, except the south wing, escaped fire damage. General MacArthur pinpointed the Imperial as his occupation headquarters and extended its life a little longer by ordering repairs to make it usable. After the occupation, it was turned back to the Japanese government. By this time repairs and maintenance would have cost unavailable millions—everything needed cleaning, restoring, renovating. The stone had weathered badly; there was no air conditioning; the heating system was antiquated, inadequate, and made unaesthetic by augmentation; and the building had settled unevenly after withstanding several major earthquakes. Parts of it were sinking quickly—an inch every three years—into the fluid mud below. Large new buildings in the neighborhood had caused changes in the underground water table, which added to the structure's instability. Demolition was both inevitable and economically reasonable.

The demolition of the Imperial Hotel was the most publicized destruction of a building since the Parthenon was blown up in 1687 by a Venetian shell aimed against the Turks, who were using the structure as a munitions dump. Committees were formed to attempt preservation, articles appeared, collections were taken up, pledges were recorded. Nevertheless the protests of architects, government ministers, art historians—and even Mrs. Wright's trip to Tokyo—could not save the Imperial. In 1967, I went to Washington, D.C., to plead with the A.I.A. and a number of foundations to preserve at least parts of the hotel. Although it was obvious the building would come down, I hoped that a foundation or museum or university or some other private organization would make plans to capture an entire room and recreate it, complete with original furniture and decorative details. It is a disgrace to the profession and a loss to the art world that nothing remains of the Imperial today but some furniture, a handful of oya stone bricks, and a small section of the building in Meiji Village, ninety miles from Tokyo.

Like the other apprentices, I had always wanted to see the building, and I felt obligated to Mr. Wright's memory to do what

Aerial view showing entire hotel and nearby high-rise buildings.

Opposite: Peacock Alley and main dining room.

Relocated and restored Imperial Hotel entrance at Meiji Village, Japan.

Detail of interior stair, with oya stone lighting fixture.

Photographs of author on visit to site during demolition and of Antonin Raymond with local architect, also on final tour.

Main dining room, broom-cleaned before demolition.

I could for the Imperial. So I went to Tokyo in December 1967, after my trip to Washington. Architect Antonin Raymond, who had worked on the early construction phase, had returned to Japan after the war. When I arrived in Tokyo, he introduced me to the hotel manager and spent a good deal of time with me.

Demolition had been under way for about a month. The guest rooms were stripped of furniture and furnishings, the plumbing had been removed, the wings were already coming down. The great public spaces, however—lobby, ballroom, dining room, and the rest—were still intact.

From my room in the "new" Imperial, a "modern" 300-room annex put up during the 1930s, I could see the progress of the demolition. By the end of my six-day stay, I'd seen the wrecking ball, swinging night and day, knock parts of the building to rubble, blow by blow.

Raymond, his wife, and I took a tour of what remained. At the entrance to the Imperial, the huge pond and the sculptures reflected on its surface were still breathtaking. I was familiar with all the rooms—and the decoration and the entire character of the hotel—from photographs and from my early experience in the Taliesin drafting room. Still I was dazzled by the intricacy, the complexity, of the design. Compared to other buildings of its time, the Imperial was an artistic phenomenon.

Our tour started with the lobby and the adjacent areas, continuing through the dining room and up to the ballroom. The theater had already been sealed off. In the Peacock Alley workmen were taking down the bronze light fixtures. The ceiling of the ballroom, restored after the incendiary nearly to its original state, was being stripped.

The Japanese are fantastic demolitioners. Before they tore the building down they broom-cleaned it. Most of the furniture had been sent to a secondhand store ninety miles away. A few old pieces were tossed out of the windows onto the rubble. A bust of the original general manager of the hotel, Mr. Hayashi, had stood in the lobby. He fared better than the furniture. They took him down from his pedestal and wrapped him neatly in gauze—he was to be set in place in the new building. I asked the manager to give me examples of every structural element—a brick, a piece of the terra-cotta, a segment of the cornice, and so on—for the architecture department of the State University at Buffalo and requested a chair for the chair collection of the college at Geneseo, New York. The chair was delivered to my room before I got back upstairs. Aside from these few artifacts—and the one portion of the hotel that is reconstructed in Meiji Village—no museum, no university, no historical society has preserved any significant part of the Imperial. By such monumental neglect, we have failed to respect history for future generations. "Daddy Frank" surely would have done something—but he'd already been gone for eight years.

View of main entrance and view of pond.

This building was Closed
on November 23, 1967.
The Grill and Prunier
restaurants have been
moved to the New Building.
The Management

当旧館は11月23日（木）をもちまして
全館を閉鎖いたしました。
長らくのご愛顧を厚く御礼申しあげます。
なおグリル、プルニエの業務は新館に移
して営業いたしております。
支配人
帝国ホテル

Sign at restaurant entrance and state of building demolition the day I left.

7

From 1916 to 1922, while the Imperial Hotel was in construction, Mr. Wright traveled back and forth across the Pacific just about each year. For his intermittent residence in Tokyo, he designed a work studio and apartment in the annex on the Imperial site—a "modest little nook" he called it. Actually it was rather elegant, complete with grand piano, fireplace, and a balcony planted with Japanese miniature trees. He also opened an office in Los Angeles, his West Coast base, and spent part of each year working there, assisted by his son Lloyd, who had become a practicing architect. During the stays in Japan, the architect Richard Schindler took charge of the California office. Mr. Wright also managed extended annual visits to Wisconsin during those years. Although his thoughts were mainly directed to the Imperial, there were other commissions—the earlier jobs to finish around Chicago and new possibilities to follow up. He left an architect, Herman V. Von Holst, in charge at Taliesin during his absences to supervise projects.

One of these jobs was a barn with a series of sheds. It had been designed for the aunts at Hillside by Von Holst. The barn had originally been built while Mr. Wright was away. Mr. Wright had never liked it. It wasn't totally in his idiom. In 1933, he had us work on extensive drawings to remodel it. The parts wouldn't form an integrated whole, so he had us demolish it. Mr. Wright had the courage to eradicate a building that didn't work out aesthetically.

Top left: The Lloyd Jones barn, still standing in 1932.

Top right: Study model that I made from Mr. Wright's design, which led to eventual demolition of the barn. Materials were rescued for use in other buildings.

Bottom: Scene in Taliesin living room on Mr. Wright's fifty-sixth birthday: the Swiss Werner Mosers (violinist and lady with infant), the Richard Neutras (cellist and man second from left), and the Japanese apprentice Kameki and wife.

Mr. Wright enjoyed changing Taliesin.
Note the fireplace hood change.

With the Imperial completed, Mr. Wright was ready to go on to new ideas. As monumental and extraordinary as the hotel may have been architecturally, professionally it was more the grand finale to an era than the promise of a new direction. After the Imperial, one would have thought California the ideal frontier for Mr. Wright. He loved the richness of the western landscape—the sea and the mountains. Californians were building everywhere, and another period of production as fruitful and varied as his Oak Park days might have seemed natural. But his trips back and forth to Japan and his long visits at Taliesin and his other travels, combined with the unhappy personal life he shared with Miriam Noel, his companion since 1914, distracted him. He never found the right combination of circumstances for his architecture to flourish in California as it had near Chicago. In no time, he often predicted California was to be ruined as a frontier, botched by realtors and bankers. And the state, as beautiful as he found it, could never have been more than an adoptive home, for home was in the Wisconsin hills where he'd grown up and then built Taliesin.

Throughout this period of travel and unsettled searching, Mr. Wright was experimenting, working on new systems and projects, but a lot of his energy went to efforts at holding his life together. Anchoring himself to the tangible, to the very materials of building construction, he managed through his art to keep strongly in touch with reality in a period when any lesser man might have given up altogether or gone mad. From the personal point of view, these middle years were intensely tragic, filled with more sorrow and disappointment, more emotional, financial, and legal troubles than many other men could ever bear. Professionally, they were years of few commissions. Those that he had were important ones, to be sure, but they were not numerous. Indeed, from 1923 to 1933 Mr. Wright saw only two projects actually constructed: the house in Tulsa for his cousin, Richard Lloyd Jones, and a summer house for his friend D. D. Martin on Lake Ontario west of Buffalo, New York, which was built without Mr. Wright's supervision. While both houses obviously reflect the Wright personality, neither has the feeling of genius.

The Jones house, in fact, is one of Mr. Wright's most uncharacteristic buildings—one without any real scale. One winter, when the Fellowship traveled from Spring Green down to Taliesin West, we stopped in Tulsa for the night. The Joneses invited us all to stay over. About twenty-five of us unrolled sleeping bags and spread ourselves all over the house. In the morning, our hosts made us breakfast and sent us on our way south. I don't think any of us really liked the Jones house. I don't think Mr. Wright did, either. (And he certainly didn't like his cousin.) The furniture seemed very skimpy, and the overall design of the house, too, seemed thin. There was an earlier scheme for it, set on the diagonal, that would have worked in a much more exciting way. As it was built, though, the plan of the outside walls was simply rows of columns, one block wide, with glass between. Jones said the stripes of light coming in made him feel like a zebra. Mr. Wright admitted that he should have weatherproofed the inside of the blocks, because each column leaked, making puddles inside when it rained.

Mr. Wright's almost complete lack of commissions in the 1920s is especially remarkable because those were years of vigorous artistic ferment and immense architectural activity, both in Europe and America. Interestingly, after World War I the nature of architectural activity in this country, at least in the Midwest, turned sharply away from its earlier directions. The bold generation of young Chicago architects who had studied and worked with Mr. Wright in the Oak Park studio—and who had absorbed so much of his thinking—declared a reversal in philosophy. They turned away from the Prairie house and went "classic"—no more original than their East Coast counterparts. It's also curious that even though there was much building being done, except during the brief depression of 1923, there were so few strong personalities in American architecture at the time.

Shortly after Mr. Wright's final return from Japan, his wife, Catherine, agreed to a divorce after more than a dozen years of separation. In 1924 he married Miriam Noel, his companion for the previous years, even though they had not been happy together. She left him after five months to "live a life of her own." Then his mother died, and also his *Lieber Meister,* Louis Sullivan.

The two men had been reconciled shortly before Mr. Wright left to work on the Imperial, and they corresponded all through the Japan years. Mr. Wright's devotion to Sullivan had never diminished, and Sullivan, in his astringent way, was proud of his former draftsman. Sullivan wrote an article praising the Imperial. Sullivan's last years, pathetic, hopeless, and disillusioned, troubled Mr. Wright and touched him deeply. His tremendous sadness about the last meeting with Sullivan—in an old, run-down Chicago hotel—showed when he told us Taliesin apprentices about it. Sullivan had been working on his *Autobiography of an Idea,* reading parts of the manuscript aloud to Mr. Wright, who visited him in Chicago from time to time. When the book was published, Sullivan, shrunken and wasted, gave Mr. Wright the first copy. The day after that visit, Sullivan died. Mr. Wright cherished the book, but could never bear to read it. One day during the Fellowship period Mr. Wright must have been thinking about Sullivan's death. He came into the drafting room and announced, "I've got to design my tombstone, because if I die before Elmslie, he'll design it in the Louis Sullivan style." Neither one of them designed the tombstone.

In April 1925 another devastating fire enveloped Taliesin,

Grave marker for Mamah Borthwick Cheney, made after Mr. Wright's death at the direction of Olgivanna Wright.

Mr. Wright's grave marker, at the family chapel, selected by his wife, Olgivanna—as it came out of the quarry. The inscription on the stained glass marker reads: "FRANK LLOYD WRIGHT, 1867–1959. Love of an idea is the love of God."

destroying Mr. Wright's copy of Sullivan's autobiography and part of his oriental art collection. The entire living area burned, though the open loggia provided a fire stop so that the drafting room and thus the drawings were spared. There was a hatch in the loggia soffit through which we apprentices would look and see the charred sheathing. The fire had been caused by a defective electrical system. Afterward there was a strong argument about how the fire should have been fought. Mr. Wright at first thought the flames could be stopped and wouldn't let a thing be removed from the house. Only at the last minute did he permit his neighbors to carry out screens, sculpture, rugs, and whatever art objects they could still reach. The piano was heaved out. When Taliesin was rebuilt, the piano ended up on the balcony above the vault in the drafting room, legless and resting on makeshift stools. I believe that Mr. Wright would probably have rebuilt Taliesin even if it hadn't burned, just for the sake of change. Never let things go stale.

In 1925, however, money for rebuilding was nonexistent. Mr. Wright already owed and was owed. With even greater determination than he'd shown after the first fire, he vowed to rebuild his domain, as though the reconstruction of Taliesin would symbolize the reconstruction of his life.

At this difficult time, Mr. Wright's focus on architecture shifted again and then expanded. To the public and to the rest of the profession, by the late 1920s Mr. Wright's practicing career seemed finished because his personal difficulties bore so heavily on his work. At the age of sixty, he was looked upon as the grand old man of architecture—a sharp-tongued critic, but a voice from a past era. While the mainstreams of architecture were busy designing, building, publishing, and creating their artistic controversies and revolutions, Frank Lloyd Wright began to think out new ideas. During the 1920s, the incredible richness and diversity of his thinking generated a more dazzling and potentially influential architecture than the preceding twenty-five years of his career. He created more new forms, new concepts of space. Many projects that he began to work on, purely theoretical at this time, became prototypes for buildings later acclaimed as revolutionary. Here, in the "unproductive" 1920s, are the seeds of the Johnson Wax Building's mushroom columns, the Guggenheim's spiral.

Mr. Wright evolved new building systems and new uses for materials. Concrete "textile blocks" in California houses, as well as skyscrapers formed by steel structure systems based on trees—all this began to take a vital form. His designs ranged from grand single-family houses to low- and middle-income housing in elegant apartment blocks, to planning for extensive rural areas, and ultimately to his Broadacre City plan—his total vision of a model city. But without real commissions, this was the period of fantasies—brilliant, bold, and often

"La Miniatura"—house of Mrs. George Madison Millard,
Pasadena, California, 1923, the first concrete block house
design by Mr. Wright.

Design for a life insurance company, Chicago, Illinois, 1924.
Right: Design for house among redwoods, same period.

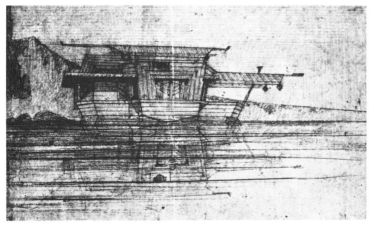

Designs for barges, for the ill-fated Doheny Ranch project that was not executed.

unbuildable. Mr. Wright claimed even to have conceived the idea for the helicopter during this period! He decided that planes, in the traditional design, were not safe. They landed and took off too fast. He thought they should slow down for these maneuvers and should also be able to do them vertically.

In later years, when there were sometimes more projects than he could keep up with, he had less time for imaginative indulgences. But in the 1920s he invented whimsies such as floating cottages and tipi cabins for a Lake Tahoe summer resort colony, and a glittering steel cathedral, some 1500 feet high, to house thousands of worshippers of all religions. He planned a sprawling southern California ranch development and undertook design projects as weighty and worldly as the National Life Insurance Company skyscraper in Chicago and a block of apartments in New York. The last two projects were more than fantasies, but the money for the apartments disappeared in the 1929 crash. St. Mark's in the Bouwerie, as the apartment tower was to be called, was the project of William Norman Guthrie, an Episcopal minister who had known Mr. Wright in Illinois twenty years earlier. Guthrie thought of buying a whole city block for his New York church and building an apartment house for revenue. He sent for Mr. Wright to design it—and then came the crash of 1929. Mr. Wright's design for the St. Mark's apartments was realized in 1952, in modified form, as the Price Tower in Bartlesville, Oklahoma.

The ideas for all these projects emerged—innovative, strong, and predictive of styles and techniques that would become standard within thirty years. Detailed drawings were made of every project, but no buildings grew up. External economics in general and his clients' finances in particular, as well as Mr. Wright's personal situation, prevented the realization of his designs. They were left on paper for the future.

Mr. Wright and friend Carl Sandburg—whose *Rutabaga Stories* Mr. Wright enjoyed—at Taliesin, mid-1920s.

Architects must be practical as well as creative and Mr. Wright, like others, was always searching for a way to beat the cost system. Progressive architects have often looked for salvation through the machine, through mass production and standardization, through prefabrication, which meant speed in construction and lower cost of materials and labor. Throughout his career, Mr. Wright created new schemes for economy in building, so that people could have better homes without being forced to pay unreasonable prices. One of his earliest attempts to provide a fine but inexpensive home for the average middle-class American family was the Fireproof House for $5000, designed in 1906 for the Curtis Publishing Company. Much later, in the 1930s, he began to develop the practical "Usonian homes," a system of "ideal houses" that the average family could afford. This system would, if widely adopted, mean better living for

Price Tower, Bartlesville, Oklahoma, 1952, included apartments and offices.

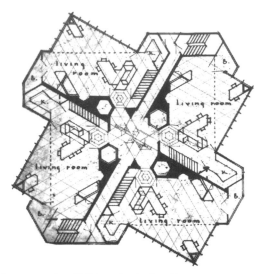

Ink tracing by apprentice Tafel made during first Fellowship winter. Plan of St. Mark's in the Bouwerie later adapted for use in the Price Tower.

Americans—an idea he kept in mind for fifty years. Mr. Wright hated lawyers, realtors, and money brokers, calling them the "real culprits." They and the unions were his enemies.

In between, during the 1920s, Mr. Wright had a romance with concrete, which he made into a poetic building material. He thought concrete would be the magic solution to innumerable architectural problems. He often told us: "Brick and stone and wood and for the most part steel—they're all straight lines. But when you get into concrete, it frees you. You can have curved lines, domes, arches, free forms, and you can pour the structure and the finish surface all at once." Here was beauty *and* economy. His use of concrete gave rise to an ingenious and original building system, a style influenced by the nature of the material. Concrete, which resembles a paste or batter that sets, is a plastic material that can be molded or sculpted or coaxed into any form imaginable. Mr. Wright said that this flexibility opened up a new freedom for design. And concrete is "honest" and durable; its production can be standardized. He was convinced that the inherent qualities of the material in a concrete building should be apparent from every viewpoint—above you, around you, on the inside and on the outside.

He had thought of working with concrete as early as 1901, when he specified it as the material for a bank project that was never built. The first project executed in concrete was Unity Temple, 1906. In Midway Gardens, he started to work out the textured concrete block approach, using a unit, or grid, system. This approach also led to the isolation of geometric decoration into panels, which architectural historians later pegged as a "Mayan influence."

Mr. Wright created panels of ornament as early as 1908 on the exterior of the Coonley house. Much later he used poured concrete at Fallingwater, in 1936, and then at the Guggenheim Museum in New York. But concrete may not be a good choice of material for the northern states. Temperature changes—freezing and thawing—are hard on it. The material checks, shrinks, and spalls. In southern states such as California and Florida, it was successful because it was compatible with the climate.

Another opportunity to do a major project in concrete came with the Barnsdall commissions in 1917: three houses plus a kindergarten, theater, and shops. (Only the houses were actually constructed.) Aline Barnsdall, the daughter and heiress of America's first oil refiner, was one of the few clients who could match Mr. Wright in wit, strength, and stubbornness. She could even outtalk him. Actually, he was a bit afraid of her, but her projects appealed to his sense of architectural romance. Miss Barnsdall, who was involved in theater, had an aura of melodrama that Mr. Wright admired—and feared.

Design for a kindergarten, made of concrete block, called the "Little Dipper," on Olive Hill, for Aline Barnsdall.

Her main house, begun in 1917, was to stand on Olive Hill in Los Angeles. Before she and Mr. Wright had even reached an agreement, she named it Hollyhock House, for sentimental reasons. He turned her flower symbol into the poetic motif for the integral ornament of the house. In a manner similar to Central American or Mayan patterns, for which Mr. Wright admitted a fascination, the stylized hollyhocks repeat around the entire building, above the windows. He and Miss Barnsdall both hoped for a lightness and playfulness in use of materials. Mr. Wright wanted the house to be like a free-form musical composition, a *romanza*. He felt it should respect the climate and terrain of California and be sincere in "sentiment"—none of the pseudostyles or periods so much in favor with eclectic Western taste. Inside the house, there were pools on either side of the hearth, with a skylight above so that and one could see the stars and the moon reflected in the water: the *romanza* element. Mr. Wright always liked the house, but he worried about its troubles. For one thing, it leaked like a sieve. Then, it was constructed in a peculiar way—poured concrete, as he had intended, but only from the foundations to the top of the windows, with stucco on wood framing above. The stucco cracked; water got in and ran down the interior walls. When we apprentices visited the house, many of us felt that the details had not been worked out sufficiently. The final effect was altogether undomestic in size and feeling— massive and ponderous. But romantic, yes. It topped a hill. What a view over the city!

In a pilgrimage one spring, a dozen of us went to see Hollyhock House. Miss Barnsdall showed us around. The house was unoccupied and unfurnished. Miss Barnsdall was living in another house on the estate. Out in the courtyard, we noticed that the landscaping was cared for and lush. When we asked how she could have given up living in Hollyhock House, she gestured to the walls and snorted, "How would you like to be damp all the time?" In designing the house, Mr. Wright wanted to stay so consistently with his grammar of concrete that he insisted on a concrete door—two inches thick. "I need three men and two boys to help me get in or out of my own house," Miss Barnsdall complained.

Formal and stark—it had been furnished in heavy furniture that looked as if it were made of bronze—Hollyhock House was more like a place than a home. It was quite a change from Mr. Wright's usual open and horizontal, elegantly sweeping architecture. Here, the heaviness of the house made it stand out from the landscape instead of blending with it in an organic and inseparable fusion. He had tried another tack.

Miss Barnsdall thought of herself as a radical, a "parlor Bolshevik," Mr. Wright called her. In the 1930s, she erected signs painted in giant letters around the base of the hill saying, "FREE SACCO AND VANZETTI," and quoting Upton Sin-

Aline Barnsdall's "Hollyhock House," Los Angeles,
California, 1917. *Top:* Living room at right. *Bottom:*
View of court.

Views of Grady Gammage Auditorium, Tempe, Arizona, 1959, with head of Mr. Wright in loggia, sculpted by apprentice Eloise Swaback.

clair, and promoting the single tax. When she came east to visit Taliesin, Mr. Wright went the forty miles to Madison to meet her train. She and Mr. Wright embraced as old friends. He teased her, "Aline, with all your money, you're just a communist at heart!" "Frank," she quipped back, "when we communists take over, I'll make you first commissar of architecture." No government would make his free spirit head of anything. Government would not commission him.

Mr. Wright would create an image of each client. He'd say to himself, "You're a wealthy client, and this is the way I think you should live." And he usually convinced them, architecturally. Most clients, especially at that time, had neither the background nor the specific knowledge to identify or program their needs succinctly. They accepted his word. He talked to the drawings as he worked, conducting imaginary conversations with the invisible client as he worked on design, saying, "Well, that may have cost $50,000, but we've just saved $10,000."

The theater he designed for Aline Barnsdall remained in the drawing stage; there was also a small plaster model. Mr. Wright's love of the stage was not to find architectural expression till later. He loved the theater so much he'd drive all the way to Madison to see anything—even a third-rate vaudeville show. It was his theater commissions, the Grady Gammage Auditorium in Tempe, near Phoenix, and auditorium commissions that largely kept the Fellowship going after his death.

It wasn't until the 1940s that his philosophy of the "new theater" was fully worked out in the Humphreys theater in Dallas. He considered the proscenium "the enemy" of the theater, preferring theater-in-the-round, with actors and audience together in the same space. In the plans for the Barnsdall theater, Mr. Wright paid no attention to the sight lines. A person sitting way over on the left would get a good view of the architecture— that's all. In this theater design, complete integration of the arts and architecture was Mr. Wright's aim—whether you saw or not. The whole was more important than the parts.

The kindergarten that was to be part of the Olive Hill complex came to a violent, or demolishing, end. Miss Barnsdall had planned to use it for her daughter and others. Mr. Wright designed it and construction was begun. When the walls were about three feet high, architect and client had one of their battles. Infuriated, Miss Barnsdall ordered the whole thing torn down, right to the foundations, and planted over.

The Barnsdall house and the two small "studio" houses were finished about 1920, while the Imperial Hotel was still in construction. After that, Mr. Wright's romance with concrete was expressed in four more California houses. In these houses, he advanced from the monolithic smoothness of the Barnsdall exterior to a fully textured surface, reminiscent of an Indian temple or a deeply brocaded fabric. Mr. Wright called this the "textile block" system. On our Fellowship pilgrimage to Hollyhock House, we also visited three of these textile block houses—the Storer, Freeman, and Ennis houses in Los Angeles. A great experience.

The textile block system was created to standardize the production of building components so that a house could be put up quickly and easily with common labor at low cost—and still be "architecture." The architecture had to grow out of the construction system, unforced and unfancied. Mr. Wright kept the threads of a textile in mind, and he began to see houses "woven" of concrete, delicately ornamented. The walls, floors, possibly even the interior partitions, could be made from concrete blocks.

Charles Ennis house, Los Angeles, California, 1923. Textured blocks with integral color. Working drawings and supervision by Mr. Wright's son Lloyd.

Mr. Wright talked enthusiastically about refining and "educating" concrete, which he called "the despised outcast of the building industry." He saw a way to make it work, by incorporating reinforcing steel into the vertical and horizontal joints. When the blocks were set in place, concrete could be poured into these joints, making a strong and earthquake-proof building fabric. Houses constructed in this manner would have double walls, a wythe of concrete block facing inside and a wythe of concrete block facing out, with hollow space between. This type of wall would be, Mr. Wright thought, an excellent insulator, keeping out the California heat and humidity. He was so convinced of the system's efficiency and beauty that many of his projects of the 1920s—some built and some not—were based on it, from modest houses in California to grand resort schemes. Thirty years later, the public would see the system copied by others around the world.

In actuality, the textile block system was less simple and less easy to put together than Mr. Wright had imagined. The block idea itself worked well, but each house required more than thirty different molds for blocks. To be workable, the system needed special corners, jambs, caps, bases, plain blocks, textured ones, some textured with stained glass inserts, spandrels, half blocks (half for inside and half for outside), and column blocks. The blocks were affected by the weather, another difficulty. After a while, the exposed surface streaked like any concrete surface.

Another problem is that textile blocks do not comfortably accommodate utilities. Each problem had to be worked out individually, sometimes at the drawing stage, sometimes during construction. The "unit system" works well on paper, where walls have no real physical thickness; but it's difficult to know where to position real walls when designing on a grid. Do they go on the center lines of the grid? Or on the edge? Mr. Wright advocated a unit construction system using a four-foot or five-foot or ten-foot module. As far back as the American System houses of 1915, he'd based nearly every project on a grid. The grid was the point of departure for design. An architect who is designing on paper, uses the grid to get a feeling of scale and space rhythm. A grid can be a checkerboard, like graph paper, or even a hexagon. Mr. Wright felt theoretically bound to stick to the system. Often he'd set up a grid corresponding to the drawing, start designing, and draw lines that went right off the grid. An apprentice standing by might say, "Mr. Wright, you just went off the grid," and he'd reply, "I'm not going to be a slave to the grid just because I invented it."

Our drawings at Taliesin—because of the grid—had the unusual architectural quality of bearing no dimensions. Floor plans are usually covered with numbers. On drawings we did for Mr. Wright, since he used a basic grid as the measure, the only dimensions to appear were those indicating something off

John Storer house, Hollywood, California, 1923. The house, neatly settled into a hillside, was supervised by Mr. Wright's son Lloyd.

the grid. For example, if he wanted an element forty feet and six inches in length, and if we were working with a four-foot unit, we'd put in ten units and merely indicate the six inches that went off the line. On the building site, it was a different story. Contractors used to wish that Mr. Wright would put in regular dimensions like everybody else. Each time the men measured something, they had to go back to the beginning and start counting up grid units. Mr. Wright wanted every drawing to be a beautiful abstraction as well as an informative document. He didn't like to see the drawing cluttered up with arrows and numbers. But he went ahead and cluttered it with his own notations.

I've often wondered who took care of him during the early 1920s. Mr. Wright wasn't the kind of man who can live alone and take care of himself. He was never totally self-sufficient. I doubt that as a child he learned to make his own bed and pick up his clothes. His mother spoiled him. No spartan living for this one—in spite of summers at the farm with his uncles and "adding tired to tired." I don't think Mr. Wright ever washed his own socks in his life. He'd leave shirts around anywhere; if he didn't have a clean shirt, he'd wear a dirty one. In Japan, like every other gentleman, he had a personal valet, but in the United States he had no servant. During those middle years, who could have looked after him? He loved to be mothered and cared for, but he had not yet found the person who was to fulfill this need.

Late in the autumn of 1924, in Chicago, Mr. Wright met the woman who was to help bring back his taste for life and work—Olgivanna Lazovich. Born in Montenegro, a small principality now part of Yugoslavia, she was the daughter of Montenegro's Chief Justice and granddaughter of a general who'd become a popular hero. She was educated first in Czarist Russia and then, in her early twenties, spent several years at Georgi Gurdjieff's Institute for the Harmonious Development of Man at Fontainebleau, near Paris. When she and Mr. Wright met, she

Mr. and Mrs. Wright visiting the Dana house in Springfield, Illinois.

was in her mid-twenties. She was in this country to complete divorce proceedings on her first marriage. The first few years of her life with Mr. Wright were difficult because Miriam Noel tried to enforce claims to both Taliesin and its master. Public opinion, the newspapers, and the law changed their attitudes in favor of Mr. Wright as Miriam Noel became increasingly vindictive and irrational. Olgivanna and he were able to marry in

1928, and within two years, when legal action stopped upon Miriam Noel's death, it seemed that an undisturbed, normal life would be possible at last for them at Taliesin. His marriage to Olgivanna was a tremendous stabilizing element for him—her devotion and strength brought his genius forward again. She knew how to take care of him. When they married, Svetlana, her daughter from her first marriage, was about seven. With Svetlana and their own daughter, Iovanna, they led a family life—something he had sorely missed for twenty years. Svetlana loved him as if he were her father, and he adored her. As she grew up, she began to twit him, to talk to him in a special teasing tone full of love, calling him Daddy Frank. In the early Fellowship days, we also called him Daddy Frank, or DF,—but never in his presence.

During those frustrating years after his return from Japan, Mr. Wright may have suffered a personal disorientation, but there was also a nationwide or era-wide disorientation. Prewar World War I effervescence gave way, after the war, to a period of frenzied hysteria in which Mr. Wright's philosophies of home, family, and culture had no place. Rather, their enduring importance was momentarily washed over by a decade or so of fashion that ended precipitately with the crash of 1929.

In the mid-1920s, one of Mr. Wright's former draftsmen from the Oak Park studio, Albert McArthur, started to design Phoenix's Arizona Biltmore Hotel. The plan was to use Mr. Wright's textile block system on an extensive scale. Possibly the job was beyond McArthur's scope. He called on Mr. Wright for advice. Mr. Wright went down to Phoenix and began work, adding the octagon room and the pitched roofs—he then took over the design. There were now two forces at work on this project: the Biltmore people (money), who set up a certain initial program, and Mr. Wright. He wanted to design a building truly made of structural concrete block, inside and out. The Biltmore people wanted to use concrete block only as a facing and decoration. The owners also wanted a huge kitchen and cavernous basements, which would have required blasting into desert rock. They began calling in other consultants and did this throughout the project. Mr. Wright, who was always guarded about the Arizona Biltmore, claimed that it got out of hand financially partly because so many outside and intrusive consultants were used. He mistrusted consultants.

While in Phoenix, he met Dr. Alexander Chandler, a persuasive promoter who had promoted an entire town not far from

SAN MARCOS IN THE DESERT   ALEXANDER CHANDLER   FRAN

Project: San-Marcos-in-the-Desert. The drawing was
displayed in the Hillside drafting room and was the
recipient of bird droppings—hence the two patches.

Phoenix about thirty years earlier and had named it after himself. Dr. Chandler's resort town was well established, and his
pseudo-Spanish-style Hotel San Marcos had been receiving
guests for years. He consulted Mr. Wright on planning a winter
desert resort for vacationing millionaires.

The purity and grandeur of the dramatic desertscape appealed deeply to Mr. Wright. When they started to plan the
resort, Mr. Wright, impressed by the setting, built an informal
"camp" to be used as headquarters for the duration of the project. He loved the climate, the cool mornings and scorching
afternoons, and he loved the desert flora. He wanted to experience living in the desert while designing. His inner eye—
inspired by the sun, the saguaro cactus, the lizards and rattlers,
the brilliant flowers, the rough mountains in the distance—began
to see, in addition to the grand hotel, a fleet of cabins like full-
sailed ships on the horizon or like a flock of butterflies alighting
on a desert rock.

With his nine draftsmen, Mr. Wright built the camp in

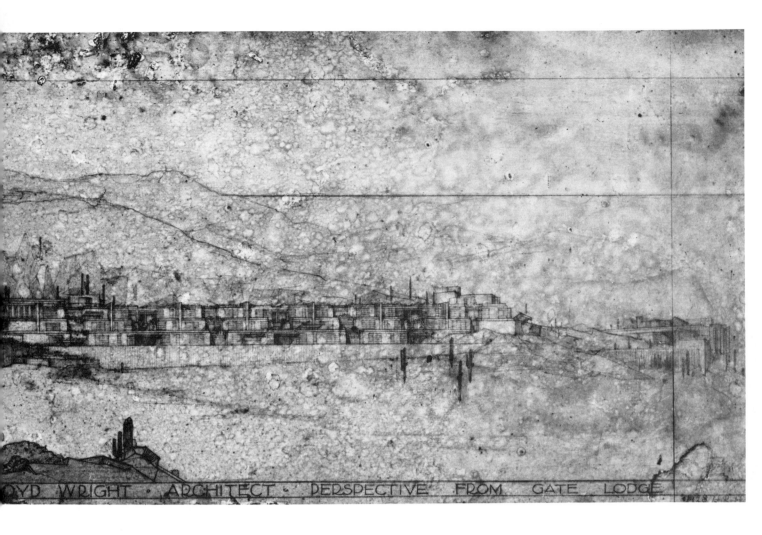

OYD WRIGHT · ARCHITECT · PERSPECTIVE · FROM · GATE · LODGE

short time, called it "Ocatilla," after the flowering cactus. Although the buildings were meant to be temporary, he designed them with the care and concern for organic beauty that went into any of his permanent structures.

In 1929, by the time working drawings were ready for Dr. Chandler, the stock market crash came and San-Marcos-in-the-Desert evaporated, leaving only a pile of plaster models for the concrete blocks. The desert camp, built of white canvas and wood, was abandoned. It disintegrated with a natural grace back into its setting. The Indians helped by stealing the materials. That was the law of the land: You couldn't leave anything in the desert and expect to find it later. Abandoned, Ocatilla was stripped by anyone who went past. We had the same problem a few years later with the first wood signs at Taliesin West. People who came along took them to use as firewood. Back East in 1929, Mr. Wright visited New York, did some writing, and began lecturing to keep food on the table. No architecture, again. Depression.

131

Never satisfied to sit quietly, Mr. Wright delighted in polemic and invective. He stirred the public and goaded the press by sounding off on any social, political, or cultural issue of the moment—even architecture. Part of the turbulence was just for fun and for the sake of drama. Being dramatic was a sure way to make the American people listen.

In the early days, from the turn of the century to the crash of 1929, architecture as an art form was given consideration by only a few—the cultured and the wealthy. The press gave so little coverage to architecture that the general public had almost no awareness of it. Perhaps this is why Mr. Wright was so intent on promoting his philosophy, why he was determined to present his ideas through all available media. He knew he couldn't spread new ideas effectively through such classical institutions as the American Institute of Architects, so he delivered lectures in the fiery and very appealing tradition of American oratory. He knew the value of architectural publicity—not only to bring in clients, but to make Americans examine their way of living. He wanted to bring them his vision of "true" democracy. This was the kernel of Mr. Wright's "mission."

Architecture, whatever else it represented for him, was the means to realize that vision. Mr. Wright never lost sight of the great ideals formulated in the Declaration of Independence. He believed that an architecture of organic direction would help the people of our country. He believed that government should pay for it. He believed that the country could afford and deserved his buildings. He never had a government commission until the very end. Mr. Wright knew where the seats of power lay, but he never lowered his standards to beg favors.

Not until the 1930s did the media in this country begin waking up to architecture—and then only slightly. Architecture did not achieve the status of a social art, with its patronage widened to include the average American, until after World War II. These days, architects must curry favor with everyone, though their clients are most likely to be committees, government agencies, and corporate boards—rather than individuals.

Architects communicate by drawing. They keep pencils handy and sketch ideas on scraps of paper as they talk. When Mr. Wright explained something, he used his forefinger, pointing in constant movement to accompany his language, as if conducting an orchestra. At the drafting table or desk he spoke and pointed while he sketched. Architects with a message know they must be able to communicate in words. Not everyone is able to follow drawings, and drawings cannot explain an entire philosophy. In writing or speaking, Mr. Wright was always eloquent.

Although he was known to have a sharp tongue, he almost always cooperated with the press or anyone who came to Taliesin to see him and talk about his ideas—anyone who asked to learn more. He was generous in making photographs and drawings of his work available from the Taliesin files. Then, too, he found ways to be published in the foreign press, because he knew that the cultured segment of the American public read foreign publications. He opened many doors to get the attention he knew he deserved.

Through books and articles Mr. Wright found one kind of audience, but he exulted in the possibility of reaching hundreds of thousands of radio listeners in the pretelevision days when all America had its ear to the radio. One winter, when he was building Taliesin West, Mr. Wright ordered lumber from a local dealer in Phoenix without having the funds to pay. For a while, the dealer pressed for payment. Some time later, he asked Mr. Wright to appear on his radio series. Mr. Wright billed the dealer in the exact sum of the lumber bill and called it square.

By 1929, his lecturing schedule kept him in the public eye—or ear—even though not many architectural commissions materialized. There were appearances in Chicago and Milwaukee, in Denver and Seattle, in Eugene, Oregon, in Minneapolis, a series of six lectures at Princeton, a week of talks in New York. A number of the lectures were published. We read the 1930 Princeton lectures as soon as they came off the press. The

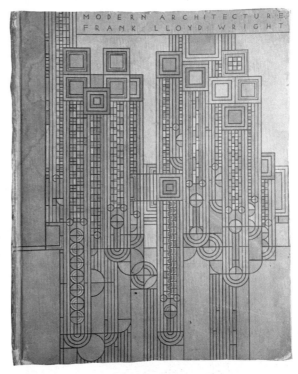

Modern Architecture, by Frank Lloyd Wright, was the title of his Princeton lectures, published in 1930. Mr. Wright enjoyed inscribing his books and always reached for a personal note.

It was not until 1938 and 1948 that an architectural magazine devoted entire issues to the master's work. Editor Howard Myers died before the 1948 issue appeared, and Mr. Wright dedicated it: "To Howard . . . with tender loving devotion to a departed friend."

book, illustrated with special drawings and designed under Mr. Wright's direction, exuded charm and grace.

He even got himself into a museum show in 1931. This was no ordinary establishment display, but the inaugural architectural exhibit of the new Museum of Modern Art in New York. The show was pioneered by Philip Johnson and Henry-Russell Hitchcock. The style of architecture was called "International"—introducing Americans to European glass and steel purity. Mr. Wright's contribution, the indigenous and organic House-on-the-Mesa, was hardly an International style sterile cube, but the exhibit brought him some attention. For the moment, he was being included with the Europeans! He felt uncomfortable, but it was exposure.

Mr. Wright delighted in finding a new audience for his ideas, and he rarely turned down a speaking engagement. He'd go off on talks to women's organizations and service clubs. Once, during an afternoon talk to the Whitefish Women's Bay Club in Milwaukee, he told an off-color story. A couple of ladies came up to him later, very insulted, to complain. The president reassured him. She said, "Mr. Wright, that was calm. You should hear the stories the ladies tell each other." He adored repeating this anecdote. He sometimes accepted college lectures at establishment institutions, where he found sponsorship for his renegade philosophies only in the student organizations. He'd get all the students on his side first, then he'd shake up the faculty, who would protest about him for the rest of the semester.

Mr. Wright was marvelous with an audience. He got a kick out of the response evoked by his more outrageous commentary. On stepping up to the podium, he would look at his audience and say, "I've seen most American cities, most of them ugly, and now that I've seen yours, I'm convinced it's by far the ugliest." Rotarians were ruffled by him. He had their attention from the very start.

All his life, Mr. Wright produced articles, gave lectures, wrote pamphlets and essays. However, his thoughts and philosophies were not organized in full-length book form until he began writing his autobiography in 1927. His writing had thus far been mostly limited to the pragmatic side of architecture. His wife, Olgivanna, now encouraged him to extend the scope of his commentary beyond organic architecture to organic living. Mr. Wright's autobiography, published in 1932, was an extraordinary work. Louis Sullivan's autobiography, published eight years earlier, was still working in Mr. Wright's imagination. Like his master, Mr. Wright wrote in the third person and emphasized his spiritual growth in childhood with rich poetic imagery, but Mr. Wright's autobiography is earthier and more vibrantly personal. He loved to play with words, often chose them for sound and not always for sense. He adored alliteration. He couldn't leave anything alone and rewrote constantly. His writing really reflected his speaking—wordy, rich, with a grammar of his own invention. Writing was his way of reaching people whom he could not reach through architecture alone. He referred to himself often as "Sullivan's alter ego," taking up his master's mission of carrying the truth forward.

The *Autobiography* made an unforgettable effect on us young people starting in architecture. Once it was in the bookstores, Mr. Wright—true to form—started revising and changing it. All through the first nine years of the Fellowship, we watched him rework it. We listened to new anecdotes and later saw many of his Sunday talks to the Fellowship turn into print. The first edition was reprinted in 1933; the second edition appeared in 1941. Soon all the available copies were sold and it went out of print. Both editions have become collectors' items, always in demand. A classic, the *Autobiography* was republished in 1977.

In the year he began the *Autobiography*, 1927, the *Architectural Record* invited Mr. Wright to prepare two sets of articles, additions to his continuing series of essays, "In the Cause of Architecture." Since his first writing commission for the *Record*, he had used this general title for all his articles. In the new series, Mr. Wright was to explain his views on the materials of architecture—brick, concrete, steel, wood, glass. He had a fantastic instinct for the use and combination of these materials and could explain how to take advantage of their individual qualities and demands.

What was so special about Mr. Wright's attitude toward the nature of materials? Today every architect knows he should be sensitive to the honest use of materials and much has been written on the subject of purity. But in Mr. Wright's early years, and even around the 1920s, architects were just beginning to explore the physical and aesthetic qualities of their materials. Before that, in classical architecture, masonry was used for every type of building meant to endure. By the end of the nineteenth century, with the stirrings of a revolution against ornamented classicism, cast iron was developed and steel followed—which changed everything.

Mr. Wright used to say—with due respect— of Sullivan, who was barely a generation older, that if the *Lieber Meister* knew the nature of materials, he ignored it. He designed the same way for stucco, stone, wood, whatever. Mr. Wright was very different: Rather than ignore nature, as he claimed Sullivan did, he tried to dominate nature. He felt that man's imprint on nature should show. This attitude explains the abstract quality of the landscaping around the Johnson Wax Building, where each planter contains a different variety of green. None of the artful "naturalism" of an Olmsted here. Nature, to Mr. Wright, was how *he* defined nature, what *he* wanted nature to do. And he honestly felt that materials would do more for him than they would for anyone else.

Addressing an audience, he drove a point home by making a fist and gritting his teeth.

135

The origins of the Taliesin Fellowship go back to Mr. Wright's family, to a strong tradition of education. Mr. Wright's father was a minister, his mother a teacher, his uncles were also preachers, and his two maiden aunts set up the Hillside Home School. He was influenced by all of this, especially by the philosophy of "modern education" that the aunts projected into their school.

The Lloyd Jones sisters vigorously ran their liberal school—with great success, but at financial loss—for over twenty-five years. The 1914 fire at Taliesin was the school's death knell. Conservative local people cruelly implied that the fire had expressed God's anger with Mr. Wright for "living in sin" with Mamah Borthwick Cheney. The scandal and notoriety discouraged many families from sending their children to the aunts' school. Old and worn out by debt, the aunts retired, giving the school buildings and 160 acres of Wisconsin farmland to their favorite nephew. They died soon after closing the school. Mr. Wright used to say that he'd promised to continue their work in liberal education. He remembered the promise later, when the depression and ill fortune had cancelled all his projects.

His career as a building architect seemed over. He thought he could become a teaching architect. He began to dream of creating a school at Hillside, in his aunts' tradition. Students could help him renovate the buildings. Tuition would pay for tools and materials. The farm would provide most of the food.

The Taliesin Fellowship would be more than a school. It would be a community for organic living, working, and learning—involving social and political theories. Mr. Wright had models to consult. He already knew about the utopian communities that were so numerous at the turn of the century. He'd visited Elbert Hubbard, leader of the Roycrofter community near Buffalo. He'd seen how the community was organized, what crafts its members practiced, what goods they produced and sold. He understood the principles underlying the community. He also knew there were more sophisticated outgrowths of the arts and crafts movement—the Werkbund in Germany and later the Bauhaus, which had been set up initially as a school for the crafts and design, where architecture did not have the central role. But Mr. Wright didn't need a model to show him how to teach architecture. He discussed the Fellowship idea often, with many of his colleagues.

The grand plan for the Taliesin Fellowship was outlined by Mr. Wright in his first prospectus, 1932, and was updated from time to time. It was originally planned to include "seven and seventy workers in the arts"—Mr. Wright, six "honor men having the status of seniors in music, painting, sculpture, drama, motion, and philosophy," and seventy apprentices. There were also to be "technical advisors" for crafts and visiting "leaders in thought" from many countries. Mr. Wright emphasized the importance of integrating work and constant contact with nature and growth. Apprentices were to live and work in buildings they had constructed or renovated using native Wisconsin materials. From the 1937 brochure: "And with a more complete consciousness of the design of the whole[,] materials are taken directly from their sources: felling trees, sawing them into lumber, turning lumber into structure, trusses, furniture, block carvings; quarrying rock and burning lime to lay the hewn stones in the wall; sculpturing them; plastering; digging; working in the field, planting and harvesting; making roads. Planning, working, and philosophizing in voluntary cooperation in an atmosphere that has the integrity of natural loveliness."

Along with these activities Mr. Wright envisioned furniture design and manufacturing; weaving; photography; printing and publication of monographs, books, music, drawings, and block prints. He planned studios for ceramics, wood, and glass and shops to sell handcrafts. He hoped to sell designs to American industry for mass production. The design force was impelling him, as always, to generate an authentic American culture. By this time, Mr. Wright had lived through the Prairie School movement and its demise, had seen the rise of a new eclecticism and the impact of people who, like Hearst, brought entire castles back to this country and of great dealers who, like Duveen, brought large chunks of European art to the United States.

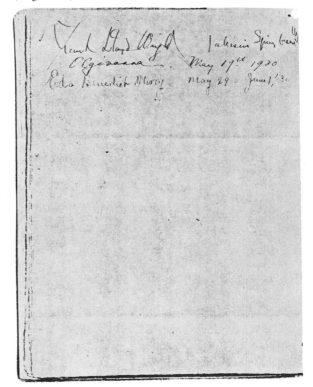

Records showing that the first Mrs. Wright and three children visited the Roycrofters in East Aurora, New York, in 1913, and (*below*) that Mr. and Mrs. Wright (Olgivanna) visited there in 1930.

During this time, you could not go out and buy "indigenous" American architecture. All you could find was colonial, which was "chintzy" carpenter's architecture. Decorators and antique dealers grabbed everything they could from Europe and brought it here because the exchange was good and there were few import restrictions.

Mr. Wright needed advice and help on the organization of daily routines for the community he was planning. For this, he turned to Mrs. Wright. In her years as a student and instructor at Georgi Gurdjieff's Institute for the Harmonious Development of Man in France, Mrs. Wright learned the patterns of living in a closed society run on a strict routine by a master with a powerful philosophy. This experience gave her the background to organize the operation of Taliesin and to bring another dimension to life in the Fellowship. In this way, her experience with Gurdjieff did influence the form of the Fellowship and some of the activities

Mrs. Wright and daughter Iovanna, with "Wolf". Fellowship gathered to bid farewell to Yen Liang, about to return to China in 1934. Bob Mosher, third from left; author (behind Iovanna) getting ready to drive with Liang to New York. The car is Liang's Model A; which he had traded for a Stutz coupe. One wonders why.

envisioned from the beginning. Mrs. Wright was the force that kept the Fellowship in working order, from the very start. A remarkable woman.

While Gurdjieff certainly had an immense and permanent influence on Mrs. Wright, the strains of his philosophy that she tried to implant at Taliesin had limited strength in the early Fellowship days. His transcendental philosophy was never one of the major currents in our life. Spiritual leanings attracted a few people to the Fellowship, but the architectural core had neither time nor inclination for an outside philosophy. From time to time, there were morning sessions for the girls with Mrs. Wright, practicing Gurdjieff's dances—patterned movements done to his own music. Later, when her daughter Iovanna went to Paris to study with Gurdjieff, there was a deeper interest in his philosophy. He first visited Taliesin in 1935.

The impressions Gurdjieff left with us were not altogether spiritual. The thing we all remembered most clearly afterward—more than his music or philosophy—was that he had taught us how to prepare sauerkraut. Under his direction, we made sauerkraut with apples—core and all—raisins, cabbage, and herbs. Health food. It was supposed to be good for us, but it was inedible. We heaped it on our plates, ate as much as we could stand, and threw the rest in the garbage can as discreetly as possible. When winter came that year, we still had mountains of the stuff in the root cellar. Mr. Wright insisted we take two 50-gallon wooden barrels of the sauerkraut to our winter quarters in Arizona. On the trip down, we truck drivers somehow got separated from the Wrights in the middle of Iowa. It had been twenty degrees below when we left Spring Green and it was still bitter cold. Looking toward the back of the truck, we saw that the barrel tops had popped off. The sauerkraut had frozen solid. We loosened the tailgate ropes and dumped the barrels into a ditch.

Later, on a visit home to New York, I went down to Romany Marie's Village restaurant, which was known for good cheap wine and colorful customers. When I walked in, I saw Gurdjieff, head shaved as always, sitting at a corner table in the back. He spotted me, pointed, and bellowed in his Russian accent, "He played my music like 'sheet'! He played my music like 'sheet'!" (I had tried to play one of his piano compositions when he visited us.) Back at Taliesin, I told Mr. Wright about the encounter. He asked me to tell him the story again and he laughed and laughed. Often as we sat working in the drafting room, he'd call out, "Edgar, what did Gurdjieff say about your piano playing?"

The sheer force of Mr. Wright's personality had more impact on the Fellowship than any philosophies or precedents. Mr. Wright *was* the Fellowship. We lived from hand to mouth at first and never had a fixed routine to cling to, but we adored him nevertheless. If we complained about kitchen duty, if we

Mr. Wright published several "square papers," distributed to his limited audience.

occasionally got on each other's nerves and acted like a pack of youngsters at summer camp, it had nothing to do with our wholehearted and wholeminded devotion to everything that Mr. Wright stood for.. Forty years later, I remember his stories clearly because I loved the man so much. And because I heard them so damned many times.

When I arrived at Taliesin that September afternoon in 1932, driven up the country road by Herbert Fritz, I knew I'd found my hero. For the time being, I was lodged downstairs, under the Wrights' wing, with about six other apprentices. Alterations were under way at Taliesin to provide more living space for the apprentices.

In the first weeks of the Fellowship, some apprentices and some of the resident workmen were put up in the Hickocks' farmhouse across the highway. The workmen soon taught us the techniques for cutting and dressing stone, for making plaster, for preparing cement. Mr. Wright had these men carrying out construction for the new Fellowship quarters, which kept them off relief. They had to be housed and fed, so he talked the county poor farm supervisor into giving us a cow for milk. He told the supervisor, "Well, we've got to get in and out of the place," and talked him into donating loads of gravel to improve the road. The phone belonged to the farmers' co-op. Mr. Wright hadn't paid his bill in a long time, so he wasn't allowed to make any long distance calls. The local service was all we were permitted to use.

Taliesin never became the close-living, totally organized community Mr. Wright had planned and spelled out in the prospectus. "Fixed hours for all, recreation and sleep." Mr. and Mrs. Wright were feeling their way at the beginning, for the first couple of years. They couldn't have had a clear idea how the Fellowship would really go.

My second day at Taliesin, I went wandering around the buildings to see what was where. There were no rules, no regulations, no one told us anything. We had to poke around and dig up things for ourselves. I discovered the drafting room. At the end of the room there was a stone vault where Mr. Wright stored, among other valuables, his extraordinary collection of Japanese prints. The top of the vault was a little balcony reached by a narrow stone stairway. I climbed up. It was only eighteen inches wide—I had to go up sideways. On this balcony stood an A. B. Chase grand piano that Mr. Wright kept in tune like all the other pianos at Taliesin. I had found a secret corner of my own. I'd been feeling lonesome, detached, and far away from New York. So I waited until no one was in the drafting room, went up the staircase to the piano and played a fugue and a sonata. Someone must have heard the music and told Mr. Wright about it, because the next day he summoned me to the living room and asked me to play. He adored music and was truly pleased to have a pianist-draftsman. When we got into the seasonal routines of Taliesin, I developed a worry about having to work with stone in the quarry and with farm machinery in the fields. I was afraid my fingers would not remain nimble enough to play the piano. Especially since I was often asked to play at a moment's notice. From time to time—while we worked in the drafting room—Mr. Wright would say, "Edgar, go up and make some music," or "Edgar, go up and play some Bach for us." He loved Bach and was especially fond of "Jesu, Joy of Man's Desiring."

Who was attracted to Taliesin? How did people hear about it? Taliesin was an extraordinary mixture of people. In addition to the architecture students and workmen, there were painters, sculptors, a few musicians, and an occasional weaver. There were also a few girls just out of high school whose folks—friends of the Wrights—thought a stay at Taliesin would do the girls some good. Why, we wondered, did Mr. Wright allow all these people to stay at Taliesin? Just to make life interesting? He liked people around him—especially if they were colorful. Many of the people who came were attracted to Mrs. Wright's philosophy and the kind of life that was being organized.

In the early days, we had a large turnover of apprentices. Life at Taliesin was not for everyone. Mr. Wright never went out and recruited apprentices, never did any advertising. Whenever he lectured, however, he'd talk about the school. And he lectured all over the country. There was some publicity in the press; however, most people learned about the Fellowship through word of mouth.

Life at Taliesin was very free, very easy, but we apprentices worked hard. At first, none of us expected to stay more than a year or two. That was my intention, and I stayed for nine. William Wesley Peters, one of the first apprentices, made Taliesin his life's work. Wes was from Indiana. His people were patriots in the Revolution, his father was a crusading editor who fought the Klan. Wes had a pioneer spirit. He was tall, burly, strong, and energetic. He came into the thick of Taliesin activities—no work was beneath him. Early on, in the first years, he fell in love with Mrs. Wright's daughter Svetlana. Their association was forbidden by Mr. and Mrs. Wright. Svetlana, seventeen years old, and Wes eloped. They lived away from Taliesin for some time, but finally returned. Svetlana and Wes were equally committed to work at Taliesin. They remained there with their two sons until Svet's life came to a tragic end. She and one son were killed in an accident on the highway to town. The other son miraculously escaped harm. Wes and Svet had lived on a neighboring farm that they called "Aldeba-

FRANK LLOYD WRIGHT

VON

H. DE FRIES

To Edgar Tafel— his nimble mind and fingers enliven our Fellowship and his spirit should make him a good architect— I hope a great one— Frank Lloyd Wright - Taliesin - when Edgar was 22 years old

Another book inscription, two years later, the last I asked him to write. The closer we worked with Mr. Wright, the less we apprentices were inclined to seek his written inscription.

Above: Yen Liang and author (left) with Eugene Masselink (right), who would serve Mr. Wright in a special creative capacity for many years.

Top left: Wes Peters (*center*), with Yen Liang and Bob Goodall.

Left: Goodall's farewell party at "Ye Olde Towne Tavern," Spring Green.

Below: "Peck's bad boy" received a telegram in later years spelling out the conditions of being an apprentice.

SPRING GREEN WISCONSIN JUNE 30 1940

EDGAR TAFEL
211 W.COOK AVE. LIBERTYVILLE ILL.

DEAR EDGAR SHOULD BE UNNECESSARY TO REPEAT. EXPECT ALL MY
BOYS HERE SATURDAY NOON TO MONDAY WHEN WITHIN RADIUS OF
TWO HUNDRED MILES.IF YOU WANT ANYTHING FROM ME CONFORM TO THE
FEW REGULATIONS IMPOSED. IF TOO MUCH I AM ENTITLED TO KNOW
REASON WHY.

FRANK LLOYD WRIGHT

ran"—star that follows a constellation. Wes was Mr. Wright's "Aldebaran."

Wes went on much later to become the chief architect at Taliesin. Not being one to have others stamp his plans, he arranged to be registered as an architect in every state in the country. Wes truly confined his life to Taliesin. He continued to live there during and after his short, much-publicized marriage to Stalin's daughter, Svetlana. Engineer and architect, Wes could calculate, zone, design any part of a project—and often did.

Some apprentices had no love of the Fellowship. They simply wanted to learn architecture the way they thought it should be taught and came for short periods. Eliel Saarinen was the only other architect who had anything like a private training center. His set-up—in Michigan—was completely different. He ran a postgraduate workshop—we called it the country club. Young architects stayed there for a year or two and went off again to practice. In no sense was it a commune. Saarinen's place had a swimming pool, tennis courts, well-kept lawns, maids and waitresses.

By the time I reached twenty-seven or twenty-eight I was very happy with the way my life at the Fellowship was organized. Partly because my work on various projects gave me an outside base, and partly because of my own independent nature, I never fell into the unreal, isolated life that characterized some of the other apprentices. Only a few of us were really outside-oriented. We had worked with Mr. Wright as architects, and with clients and contractors—all the realities of the trade. We had our individual lives too. So, I had an outside view, as much of an outside view as one could get at Taliesin. If it hadn't been this way, I would not have been able to stay as long as I did.

Among the apprentices at Taliesin was a group we called the "Know Nothing Party"—they had nothing to do with architecture and didn't seem to be doing much of anything else. They were paying apprentices who didn't get involved in anything more serious than gardening. We all started out as paying apprentices, but in 1932, after we'd been at Taliesin for just a few months, a nationwide "bank holiday"—suspending all banking functions—was imposed. Most of the parents were affected by the Depression and couldn't afford the fees even after the banks reopened. Mr. Wright never sent anyone away. He went on lecture tours. He wrote and received royalties on his books. And from time to time, new apprentices brought in new money. In those days, Mr. Wright didn't have a bank account. He paid cash—when he had the money to buy things. Whatever money he kept on hand was jammed into his pocket, a crumpled wad of notes mixed with checks, scraps of paper, and notes. He used Wisconsin State scrip for a while. Because many banks were closing, when I got a check from home, I'd take it to the bank and exchange it for scrip and silver.

Four of us horsing around for no reason.

Mr. and Mrs. Wright made attempts at organizing daily life at Taliesin, but only the meal schedules worked. The routine of no routine—that was life at the Fellowship. We dealt with each day's important matters as they came up, though the long-range building projects were handled more systematically. In spite of Mr. Wright's habit of happily disrupting schedules, certain routines were established in an organic way, dictated by the cycles of nature—planting and harvesting seasons, work outdoors until Wisconsin's winter drove us inside. Intertwined with all activities was work in the drafting room. There were always more things to do than hands and money to get them done. Winter always came too soon. Summer always came too soon. Time and the seasons were always against us, and we were always behind. Mr. Wright felt that time was pushing him, that it was behind him trying to overtake him, and that we'd never be finished. As a result, he projected that kind of frenzy onto us. Always.

The big bell rang first at 6:30 A.M. to wake us, the second bell at 7:00 called us to breakfast. We had to be in the dining room before 7:30, when the kitchen closed. If we missed breakfast, we had to beg food from Mabel, the cook, or steal something from the kitchen when Mabel turned her back. Breakfast was impressive farm fare: fresh fruit, prunes, apricots, tomato juice, cider, cereal cooked or dry. Mr. Wright liked oatmeal best, so oatmeal was usually the cereal. Then we had eggs and bacon or ham or country sausage, plenty of homemade bread and muffins, with honey or jam, jelly or store-bought peanut butter. Our coffee was boiled in a big pot, with a couple of eggshells thrown in "to settle it." In the very beginning, servants worked in the kitchen,

Photos taken when Henry-Russell Hitchcock visited Taliesin to gather material for his forthcoming book on Wright, *In the Nature of Materials,* in 1937. Bob Mosher and I were detailed to find drawings from the files. Mr. Wright constantly changed the dates on drawings. *Right:* From that same roll of negatives— author in drafting room.

took care of the linens, and served us at the tables. However, the Wrights soon found that they couldn't afford this service. So we all took turns in the kitchen helping Mabel, waiting on tables, and cleaning up. Those of us who'd attended summer camp took to it well enough; the rest had to learn.

Mr. Wright's approach to food was straightforward and simple, like the samplers with homey sayings that he hung on all the walls at Taliesin. We went to an open counter to get our food. No choice, no menus. We washed our own dishes after eating. That was the only sane way to run the place. The Wrights didn't usually eat with us. They had their own dining room, small and beautiful. From there, one could look across the crown of the hilltop, past Mr. Wright's bedroom, out into the valley. Very occasionally, a visiting parent and apprentice would be invited to eat with the Wrights.

After breakfast, duties were assigned, some continuing from days before, some new. For some time we operated by a "boss system." One apprentice would be the senior boss for two weeks, with a junior boss working under him. The senior boss would make out a list of what Mr. Wright wanted done and go over it with his assistant. Two apprentices to go over to Hillside, a few others to clean the windows, someone to drive the tractor, someone to run the road grader. The trick was to find the people to get these tasks done. People tended to disappear, to hide in closets. At the end of two weeks, the assistant moved up to become senior boss. Good training.

By 8:00 A.M. we reported for work. We might do a dozen different jobs in the morning—garden for a while, drive the tractor for road grading, dig a ditch or trench for footings to go under a new wall, drive down to the river for a load of sand, help rescue a car that was stuck. The cars often got into trouble on the dirt roads. When spring thaws started, deep ruts would form

and it would take a tractor to drag the cars free. One of the toughest and coldest jobs in winter was to cut ice in the river and haul the blocks to the icehouse, where we packed them in layers, sawdust between the blocks. There was plenty of sawdust from our own sawmill.

When a new apprentice arrived, one of us was sent to the station to pick him or her up. The affluent ones came in their own cars, which caused parking problems, so we built additional parking areas. Going to Spring Green to meet a train was a welcome break. There were two trains, the 2:30 P.M. and the 8:30 P.M. from Chicago via Madison. Practically no one came from the other direction, Minneapolis. In the evening, we'd set our watches by the 8:30 train, which tooted on the way into town. If we wanted to catch the early train to Chicago, at 3:30 in the morning, we called the station master well ahead of time and he wired instructions to have the train stop.

In spring we plowed and planted, fixed the buildings, trying to stop the leaks, cleared up the dead leaves with rakes. Mrs. Wright would be busy with her flower garden. It was wonderful at last to throw open the windows, sealed up all winter, and let in fresh spring air, even if it was still cold. More visitors would start to come, especially on weekends.

In summer we cultivated the crops in the big garden on the side of the hill. The crops were nearly enough to feed all of us, with enough left over to sell some of the vegetables. Mr. Wright would get into his Cord, fill it with baskets of tomatoes and string beans and peas, and drive to Madison to try to sell them. Trouble was, everyone else was also trying to sell tomatoes and string beans and peas, and he never got a very good price. August was the month of flies. Flypaper hung abundantly, flyswatters all over the place. Mr. Wright enjoyed swatting flies.

By August we had settled into our weekend activities with some regularity. Saturday was cleaning-up day at Taliesin, washing windows and sweeping. We gathered varieties of flowers and arranged them everywhere. Even in the drafting room. In the evening we went over to Hillside, where dinner was served in the theater. One or two people stayed at Taliesin in case of fire or other emergency. After dinner there was entertainment—the chorus sang, there were a few piano selections, and we'd have a foreign film.

Gene Masselink, Mr. Wright's secretary, would show him a list of films from which he could order. He'd look up and down the list before deciding. Finally he'd say, "Well, Gene, how about *Stagecoach*?" We must have seen that one twenty times. And *Sous les Toits de Paris* by René Clair. Those were his favorites. We saw the film in the theater at Hillside on Saturday night; the public could see it there on Sunday afternoon with coffee, for a fee. Often on Monday, when we were working in the drafting room, Mr. Wright would come through announcing, "We're going to have the film again"—which meant we had to go.

For some reason we could never figure out, Mr. Wright fixed the screen so that when films were shown, the sound track was also visible, running down the left side of the picture. Apprentices ran the projector. I managed to stay away from it. Once you were trapped into running the machine, you never got out of the duty again. After the film, Mr. Wright would turn on the lights and see that many of the apprentices had disappeared. Looking around, he'd ask, "Now, where's John?" or "Where's Bob?"

At night, if we tried to drive away from Taliesin using the front way, the Wrights could hear us going. But one could leave by the back road. Sometimes we "borrowed" one of the trucks. We'd push the truck to the back hill, get in, and roll down by gravity almost to the bottom. Near the bottom, we'd put the truck in gear and drive into town, where we'd park—not at the bar, but behind the lumberyard, hiding.

On Saturday nights a few of us went to dances in little towns around Spring Green. The dance halls were respectable, with live jazz bands; girls could come unescorted and not feel out of place. All farm community. We'd pay admission, buy beer there, or drink our own whiskey. One time, after drinking more than our usual amount of liquor, we convinced the Chinese apprentice, Yen, to get up in front of the band and conduct. The farmers were intrigued to see a Chinese conducting jazz. There were barn dances, too when a new barn was put up. On those occasions, there was hillbilly music, the real thing, with wild country fiddling.

On Sunday mornings some of the Catholic apprentices attended mass in Spring Green. Mr. Wright never made any serious attempt to incorporate religion as part of our life at Taliesin. One summer, however, he decided to open up the little family chapel in the valley. He announced that we were having Sunday church services and invited the Madison clergy. The service consisted of an organ piece played on the harmonium, a vocal solo, a choral interlude, and a sermon by an Episcopal minister, a Unitarian, a Methodist, a Rabbi (whoever was available). When Mr. Wright ran out of denominations, he decided to have each apprentice give a sermon. Mr. Wright chose the topic, which was usually the trait or quality he felt the apprentice lacked. "Kindness" was my topic. It provoked both self-analysis and apprehension as my Sunday drew near. Fortunately for me, this Sunday was extremely hot and the air in the chapel was heavy and still. Mr. Wright suggested, which was his way of commanding, that the service be held on the lawn instead. He made some pertinent remarks and announced that I would speak on kindness. I started, but after four or five sentences, I saw Mr. Wright begin to tap his cane idly against the side of his

Picnics—Mr. Wright loved picnics as a change of pace.
Top left: with Dankmar Adler's daughter. *Top middle:*
With his younger sister, Maginel.

shoe. A sign of boredom. "Well, Mother," he said to Mrs. Wright, "I think we'll go . . ." The church service disintegrated, and I was grateful not to be on stage.

On Sunday morning when there was no chapel—in spring, summer, and early fall—by about 11:00 or 11:30, we'd assemble in the tea garden for a picnic trek. The cooks had already prepared everything—their homemade cakes were especially good—and we had salads and cans of milk, homemade ice cream, our own butter and buttermilk. We'd pile into five or six cars and drive out through the valley until Mr. Wright found a spot he liked. Always a new place. He'd go up to a farmer and ask permission for us to have a picnic on the hillside. Everybody went to the picnics. (No one could get out of it.) Once, when Mr. Wright found a spot on the very top of a hill, an apprentice asked, "Why don't we eat down below and carry the food up in our stomachs?" After we were settled, Mr. Wright would say a few words of wisdom and then we had lunch. After eating, we'd split up into groups of friends, those we were talking to at the

More picnics. With daughter Iovanna. Picnic on his newly built terrace overlooking the valley. Mrs. Wright, left, and a string quartet.

More picnics. With longtime German architect friend
Erich Mendelsohn, above.

Top: Tea with guests and Mrs. Wright (right) at Taliesin tea circle.

Bottom: Mr. Wright listening to friend, landscape architect Jens Jensen. They argued incessantly about the nature of nature—Jensen was a true naturalist.

moment. About 1:30 or so, we drove back to Taliesin. The afternoon was given over to visitors, at "fifty cents a head." Each week, a few apprentices would serve as guides. The rest of us had the afternoon free, until about 6:00 P.M., when we were all invited to the Wrights' for an aperitif, a glass of wine, followed by dinner in their living room.

Our first experience with wine at Taliesin was a disaster. We made a huge batch of wine in the first year of the Fellowship, had a bit too much, and ended up on the roof. Next morning, Mr. Wright called us together and asked who'd had more than one glass of wine. We all stepped forward. He asked who'd had more than two glasses and quite a few apprentices took another step forward. Then he said, "More than three?" Four of us advanced still further. He fired us on the spot, saying he had to set an example for the others. He took us back to his office, gave a lecture on organic architecture, told us to mind our ways and stay.

On Sunday evening, people usually came to visit, editors from Madison or other newspapermen. There were also weekend guests from Chicago, sometimes clients. Everyone—clients, guests, apprentices—treated Mr. Wright as if he were a king. After dinner, the musical apprentices performed, usually playing Mr. Wright's favorites. I'd be asked to play "Jesu, Joy of Man's Desiring" and a Brahms Intermezzo. Sometimes I'd squeeze in a Debussy prelude, which he didn't really like.

One morning, after a long evening in town, several of us had monstrous hangovers. My eyes were so red I decided to wear sunglasses all day. No sooner had I emerged from my room than Mr. Wright came bounding along. "Edgar," he said with surprise, "what's the matter with your eyes?" He lifted the sunglasses as he questioned me. Looking at my bleary eyes, he said sternly, "Young man, come with me," and marched me through the loggia, through his bedroom, and into his bathroom. He opened the medicine chest, reaching for something I couldn't identify. "What you need is a tablespoon of castor oil," he said, shoving the spoon into my mouth before I could protest.

On Monday morning we apprentices reported to the drafting room. More often than not, we were soon interrupted in whatever we were doing. We were natural targets whenever someone was needed to aid in a work crisis.

When fall came, we had corn husking. Right down the lines, row after row. How beautiful the hillsides looked. The corn stalks would be cut and stacked up in little domes outside to dry. Throughout the field were little white pullets. From the distance, from the top of the hill, they looked very picturesque. These chickens had a practical use too. We used to catch a few, twist their necks, slit their throats to drain them, and hang them upside down in the corn stacks till evening. At night we'd come back to retrieve the chickens. We'd take them to our rooms and

Paul Robeson visits the Fellowship after giving a concert in Madison, Wisconsin. He spent the day singing for us and enjoyed seeing our work. November 1935.

roast them in the fireplaces; they were delicious washed down with wine or beer. At night we occasionally got eggs from the chicken coops; we boiled them over the fireplaces. Mr. Wright used a handy device for the chicken coops: doors one could lift to reach in for the eggs from a corridor in the rear, without disturbing the chickens.

Autumn tasks meant preparing for winter. The apples had to be brought in, and we made our own cider. We filled the root cellar with vegetables. We began to keep fires going in the fireplaces, until it got cold enough to turn on the boilers. There was a marvelous earthy aroma—inside and outside—of burning oak logs all through the winter. In addition to the farmers who worked at Taliesin, there were always one or two apprentices who had a farm background. They were the ones who got up at 5:00 A.M. to milk the cows. In winter they used kerosene lanterns. The garbage and swill went to the pigs. We learned that pigs don't like banana peels and won't eat orange rinds, preferring pieces of stale bread. We learned what to save for

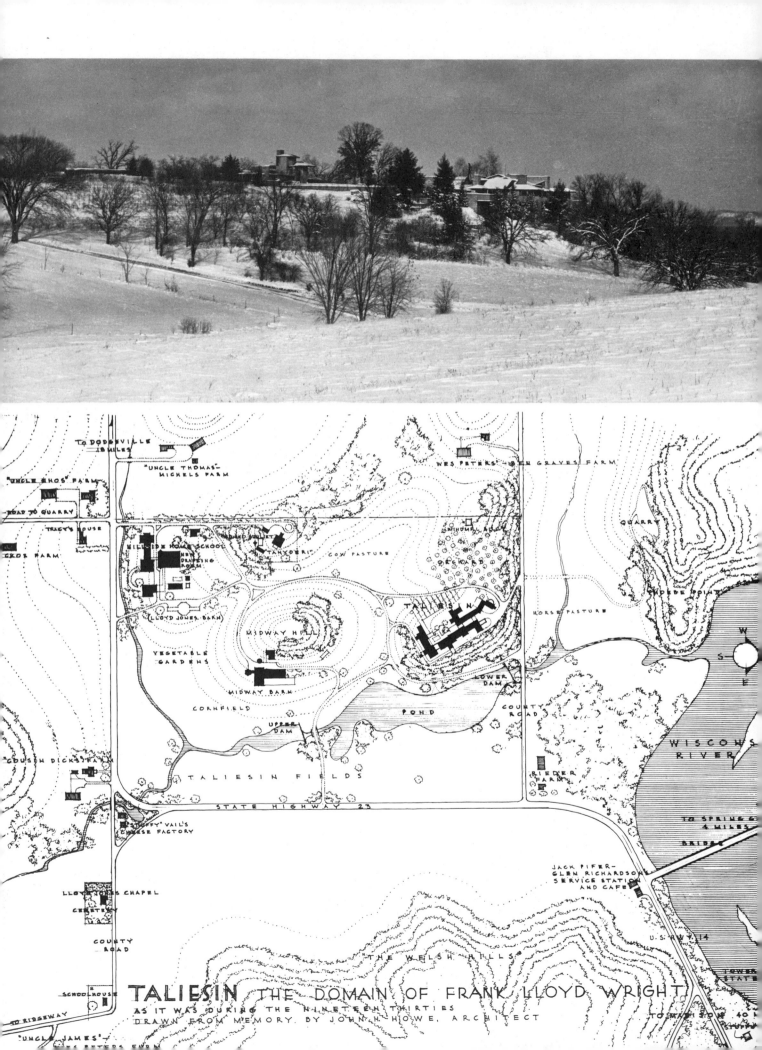

TALIESIN THE DOMAIN OF FRANK LLOYD WRIGHT
AS IT WAS DURING THE NINETEEN THIRTIES
DRAWN FROM MEMORY BY JOHN H. HOWE, ARCHITECT

Hillside original buildings constructed in 1901. Two studios were soon added and these were remodeled during the 1930s, when a drafting room and sixteen apprentice rooms were also built. The original buildings' diagonal leaded glass was replaced with plate glass, which Mr. Wright persuaded the Pittsburgh Plate Glass Company to donate. He also persuaded the Ludowici tile people to furnish roofing tiles. We apprentices uncrated and installed the materials, to learn the techniques involved.

The Hillside Home School's gymnasium was altered to a theater, with a flat floor. After a fire in the later 1940s, Mr. Wright rebuilt the theater and dropped the stage. The abstract-design curtain in the top view is made of monk's cloth with appliquéd multicolored felt.

Exhibited wood model of early unexecuted building. Wright-designed concrete sculpture from Barnsdall House . . . fragment of Midway Gardens figure . . . *right,* Chinese sculpture.

View of large Taliesin drafting room. Building this, we apprentices furnished much of the labor. We dug foundations, brought sand from the river bottom, felled trees and cut them into lumber, burned the lime and mixed plaster, laid the roof, did all millwork, built the furniture, laid the floors, stained the trusses, did finished grading, and cleaned away the debris.

Left: Midway barns in the landscape; apprentices working in the truck garden in contoured areas.

Right: Making a low spot passable for a picnic.

Below: Everyone pitched in at harvest time: hay bailing—Mrs. Wright at far right. *Lower left:* Mr. Wright at controls of threshing machine. He also enjoyed running the road grader. Author driving tractor.

them and what to discard as unusable garbage. Then there were the peacocks. Mr. Wright bought three colored peacocks and a white one—they walked freely on the roofs and screamed their awful shrieks. We also had goats and goats' milk for cheese. A big white cotton bag used to hang in the kitchen, separating the curds for cheese. This was the real organic life. We were close to nature all the time.

We struggled, learning. To me, a city boy with a carpentry shop in an apartment, getting wood meant simply going to a local lumberyard and buying what I needed, neat boards in uniform size. It was all different now, at the source. Those first winters, we took turns going to the woods to cut trees for building lumber. Mr. Wright bought his wood from neighboring farmers, "on the stump." We helped fell the trees and we trimmed the branches. Logs would be snaked to the road, rolled up on to a flatbed truck, trundled to Hillside, and dropped on the uphill side of the sawmill. We helped the professional sawyers hump the logs along with big tongs and lug away the lumber as it came from the saw—beams, framing studs, planks, boards. Bark slabs were cut in two-foot lengths to stoke the boilers and fireplaces. We sawed our own lath.

The wood came dripping wet from the mill, oozing sap; it had to dry out before use. But lath had to be wetted before it could be plastered, so why not use the wood green? Nature had soaked it for us. Do it all in one operation, said Mr. Wright. It didn't work. The lath twisted as it dried. Many walls had to be redone.

We worked the quarries—limestone for Taliesin, sandstone for Hillside, cutting out the blocks or sawing or splitting them loose, cleaving them to building size. Flat hewn stones, varying in size and thickness—ashlar. To bed the stones there had to be lime mortar, since cement was too expensive. Mr. Wright always had stone laid on its bed; the way it came out of the quarry, it went into the wall. Organic.

In that first rough winter, often twenty degrees below, we established three-day rituals to produce lime for our plaster. With one workman in charge, we built a lime kiln, an arch of limestone about five feet high and more than twice as long, with a makeshift flue at one end. For three days and nights we'd stay up there, burning the stone, keeping the log fires burning. Meals and coffee were brought from the kitchen. When the arch cooled, we took it down and hauled the stones to Hillside. There we placed them in large, shallow wooden boxes, slaked them with water for days, hoeing back and forth every so often. An organic recipe for lime to use in plaster or for bedding stones. Obtaining sand was much simpler. We just dug it out of the river bed.

We made almost everything in the carpentry shop—cabinets, shelves, trim, doors, windows. Casement windows, because

Author feeding the lime kiln fire. Half wet and half dry logs were used. Mr. Wright inscribed the back of the photograph; "That stones may be bedded, walls plastered—Firing the imagination! (The lime kiln)"

Mr. Wright hated double-hung windows and always referred to them as guillotines. Workmen came and went, for pay was scarce in the middle of the Depression. We had to learn quickly from the plumbers and electricians, so we could do piping and wiring ourselves. If the toilet got stopped up, we knew how to fix it. We had to know. We learned to do whatever needed doing. Some of us learned a lot about tractors and cars. Others were especially interested in the farm, crops and animals to care for. One day, Mr. Wright asked an apprentice to "slaughter a pig." Not knowing how to slaughter an animal, the apprentice went and got his revolver. (In those days it was not uncommon, in the Midwest, to own a gun.) After several near misses, he gave up. A workman finally came over and slit the sow's throat properly. My jobs were cutting stone and laying walls, and I loved driving the truck, the tractor, and plowing, but only for a while.

In those first days there were two of us to a room, but later most of us had our own rooms and a little time to personalize our domains. Every so often, Mr. and Mrs. Wright would make a tour to see how we had designed our living spaces. If my room happened to be a mess that day, as it usually was, Mr. Wright would call me in. Someone would say, "Edgar, Mr. Wright wants to see you in his office." I'd go at once, fearful and anxious. Sometimes the reprimand was short. If he was good and angry, the lecture took longer. In any case, it always seemed to end with a few remarks about organic architecture. We quickly learned to turn away his anger by slipping in a question about Oak Park days. This lengthened the lecture but made it more enjoyable.

Mr. and Mrs. Wright had a deep concern for the apprentices, and there was plenty to worry about, for many knew nothing about country ways or hazards. It's amazing that there were not many serious accidents. Apprentices were forever falling off horses, out of trees, down steps, off tractors, breaking arms and legs, driving into ditches, cutting themselves on saws, hammering their fingers, overeating, undereating, overdrinking.

After dinner, unless we were busy working on a project in the drafting room, our time was our own. Lights went off about ten at night—when the power was cut at the hydroelectric plant. After that it was candles and kerosene lamps. In the early days before we had public electric power, electricity was generated from the hydro machine at the dam below Taliesin. The machine didn't work very well when a turtle got caught in its turbines. An auxiliary Kohler plant supplied daytime power for the refrigerators.

Descriptions of apprentices out in the fields or making concrete or milking cows or driving the tractor, probably make it seem that little was being done in the drafting room—that architecture, the real purpose of the Fellowship, was giving way to

Apprentices, working on the roof and lugging "mud" for plastering. We also plowed out the snow with the road grader, mended fences, and did outside chores when weather permitted. After the first winter, Mr. Wright redesigned the fencing system, installing Western cattle guards and electric fences—thus enhancing the landscape.

farming. During the first three years or so of the Fellowship, there actually wasn't much to do in the drafting room. The only real project was the Willey house. Jobs did not start coming in until about 1936. Mr. Wright felt in those early years that he was getting ready. He had infinite faith that the Fellowship would grow into a working organization, that the nation's economy would revive, and that he would have created architects to build for the revitalized nation.

Left: This photograph, by Hedrich-Blessing, was taken during the preparation of the 1938 issue of *Architectural Forum.* Behind Mr. Wright is California architect John Lautner; to Mr. Wright's left are Bob Mosher (now Byron K. Mosher of Marbella, Spain), myself, and Wes Peters.

Top and middle: My photographs, taken at the same time. At top, Kenn Hedrich, photographer. The middle picture shows John Howe, now a successful architect in Minneapolis. *Bottom:* Mr. Wright, always thinking.

n the drafting room, as elsewhere at Taliesin, we learned by doing. In the beginning, with senior draftsmen to supervise, Mr. Wright had us copying drawings of his early buildings and working on drawings for the rooms under construction at Hillside. In a sense, it was a make-work program.

When I arrived, the drawings for the Hillside drafting room had just been completed. I was assigned to copying rooms of the Imperial, to making plates showing the hotel's layout and furnishings. We never knew when Mr. Wright might come into the drafting room. Any time, any day. For him, there were no Saturdays or Sundays or holidays. The drafting room was his center of everything. We'd be working, seated on benches covered with animal hides, and suddenly the door would creak. We could tell it was Mr. Wright—he always cleared his throat before entering. We stood up out of deference; those who were standing turned to face him. It was always an emotional and sometimes even an electrifying experience to have him there. Those sharp eyes!

To reach his office, he had to walk through the drafting room—but he could never walk straight through. He'd stop at drafting tables to review the work, to make additions and changes. To go back to his quarters, he had to walk through the drafting room again. When the bell rang for lunch, he often kept right on working. Daughter Iovanna might run in and pull at his sleeve, saying, "Daddy! Mommy says you're to come for lunch!" There were times when he threw down the pencil, declaimed, "I have just snatched victory from the jaws of defeat!" and stomped off.

He never thought he'd left something to be completed later. His work was always final—that was it. Later, he'd come back and change the design, making it final again.

Mr. Wright had a formidable power of concentration. Yet he'd occasionally grow restless. After drawing for a while, he might go over to the bench next to the fireplace and lie down, his cane beside him, maybe a book under his head. An apprentice in the drawing room would put a finger to his lips and warn the others not to make a sound: Mr. Wright was napping. He'd wake with a start—he never got up sluggish—and storm back to his work. Sometimes he'd change everything on the drawing. His preliminary drawings for a project were filled with lines. Sometimes he'd throw away the drawing—push it aside and let it drop on the floor.

Mr. Wright was marvelous to work with. His sense of mission permeated his thinking and the drawings that he spread out before us—ever repeating that the better world will grow out of better creative solutions, better design. Each time he sat down at the drafting board, we sensed the power of his intent. "Every change is for the betterment," he'd tell us reassuringly. He always felt he was right. Yet he always changed everything. A perpetual state of flux. "The last change is made when the boom comes down," he'd snort. Each day we feared that he'd change what he had settled the day before. We'd point out as he started revising a drawing, "But Mr. Wright, yesterday you decided it *this* way!" His answer was standard. "That was all right yesterday, but it's not right today." He never left anything alone. He no sooner got a system going than he'd upset it all. We'd be working on a project in the drafting room when he suddenly decided to decorate a room with branches. He would send the nearest apprentice off to the woods to collect foliage.

"How did we ever get anything done?" we often wondered afterwards. Mr. Wright was such a driving perfectionist. With his incessant desire to make everything perfect, he'd say, "Yesterday wasn't as perfect as today." He had a remarkable memory for the instructions he'd given us on drawings. If we drew a detail that differed the least bit from what he'd asked for, he caught it immediately. He couldn't tolerate the slightest mismeasurement or faulty coordination. Mr. Wright would not waste much time on people who were not imbued with his ideas.

The only photograph in Mr. Wright's studio of a building by another architect was one, about twenty-four inches wide, of the Potala (the Dalai Lama's residence) at Lhasa, in Tibet. He must have felt both pangs of jealousy and admiration for this structure, completed in the early 1600s, which rose from the plain to a great height.

We got to meet and know Mr. Wright's children. He had four sons: Lloyd and John, architects, David, a businessman, Llewellyn, a lawyer. They visited occasionally and were received with great warmth. Daughter Frances, who helped start

Houses Mr. Wright designed for his sons. *Top:* David Wright house, Phoenix, Arizona, 1950. *Bottom:* Robert Llewellyn Wright house, Bethesda, Maryland, 1953.

America House, a crafts museum in New York, and Catherine, married to an advertising man in New York, also came. Lloyd seemed the favorite; he was also the most abrasive and argumentative—maybe Mr. Wright goaded him into it. After he'd visited for a few days, Lloyd and his father would be at each other tooth and nail about design in the studio. "Lloyd, you just don't know anything," Mr. Wright would say. (Later, David and Llewellyn had their Dad design houses for them. Lloyd remodelled Unity Temple and the Barnsdall House—after Frank Lloyd Wright's death—with the aid of his architect son, Eric, who had been an apprentice under his grandfather and who enjoyed a dear and close relationship with Mr. and Mrs. Wright.)

A characteristic scene was played each time Lloyd came to visit. First, Mr. Wright gave him a huge welcome. Lloyd would enter the drafting room with his father and Mr. Wright would lead him from one table to the next, showing him drawings. They'd sit down at a drafting table and start to examine one of the drawings in detail. Quiet. All of a sudden, Lloyd would cry out, "Dad! How can you do something like that!" pointing to a detail in the drawing. "You know better than that!" And he'd look around and ask, "Where's a pencil? Let me have a pencil." We weren't sure what to do, so we did nothing. Mr. Wright was glaring at us as if to say, "Don't let him have that pencil." But he always found one. Mr. Wright would grab the pencil out of Lloyd's hand. "Here, let me have that. Move down, son, move down," and he'd shove Lloyd (who was about forty-five at the time) to one end of the bench. "We'll see later what to do about this."

He'd start to think aloud about this change and that, rewording the very suggestions he'd just repudiated from Lloyd. Vigorously, he'd erase parts of the drawing, his arm moving rapidly. He made changes. Next day, Lloyd would come back into the drafting room and say, "Dad, really, I just don't understand how you can do that." By the end of that day, Lloyd's presence would no longer be welcome.

All of us had to be very delicate in stating opinions to him. Sometimes he'd grit his teeth and roar. Mr. Wright was forever looking for the rule so broad that it anticipated all possible exceptions. Now, after all these years, I have some perspective and understand him better—I understand his disdain for trivia, for the hangers-on, for the non-doers. I can see how hard it must have been for him to think out the great new creative projects. One apprentice claimed that he overheard Mr. Wright say very softly to himself—while working in the drafting room—"I'm a genius." (He was designing the Rogers Lacy Hotel in Dallas, the one with the open central core.)

Mr. Wright was the strict overseer of the drafting room. The more experienced men who had been working with him before 1932 left after a few months of the Fellowship, and he was the only one there to teach us, with his supervision and critiques. We watched him draw, then tried it ourselves. It wasn't like the classic master-disciple method; we could interrupt and ask all the questions we wanted. Sometimes we left architectural magazines open for him on the drafting tables. He never suspected we were tricking him into a reaction. At least, he never let on. We learned how to evoke Mr. Wright's better nature. If a detail in a drawing didn't work, the best way to get his help was to say, "Mr. Wright, I'm in trouble. I can't get this detail to work out right." He'd sit down and muse over it, humming and singing to himself. "Let's see, let's see . . . Well, not so much of a problem. We'll fix it."

Mr. Wright and apprentice John Howe, in the Taliesin West drafting room. Photograph taken by former apprentice John Aramantides, now of Athens.

He revelled in the opportunity to show us young people how clever he was and how fast he could draw. He loved playing papa to us—in an architectural way. Mr. Wright wasn't outwardly affectionate. He was surprisingly cool—never put an arm around an apprentice's shoulder, never really touched us. In criticizing an apprentice's work, he could be devastating. To an architecture student even the gentlest critique often registers like a thunderbolt.

Mr. Wright had very little tolerance for work done in his style, in imitation. We presented drawings to him in his birthday box—he quickly passed by any that were too close to his own style of design. Whenever someone copied him, he'd tell the following story about an old butler who hated his master though he'd worked for him for years. Every morning the butler prepared the master's coffee. He would spit in it, then stir it. That's how he got even with the master. Mr. Wright used to say, "If you copy my work, it's like spitting in my coffee."

He had great praise for original work. In the drafting room, he'd sit down at the table, look over a drawing, and say, "You have an idea here." That's what he was looking for—ideas. First thing we knew, he'd reach for an eraser and change a detail. He'd say, "No, no, no! I didn't mean THAT!" He'd grab a pencil, draw, and break the point. We were always ready with freshly sharpened pencils. (That was before we had automatic pencils.) Sharpening pencils was a very special ritual to him. He took great care to teach us how to do it properly. "Hold the pencil toward you," he'd say. He loved the mingling of the two aromas—graphite and cedar. It was said that in pre-Taliesin days Mr. Wright used to go around the drafting room picking up graphite shavings from the pencils. He'd go into his office and put the shavings in his hair, which was just starting to turn gray. Soon, though, the shavings would sift out and filter down onto his collar and shirt. By the time we got to Taliesin, his hair was white. He had made peace with it.

In spite of Mr. Wright's love of theatrics, there were times when we could get him to talk seriously and give us a straight opinion. But not for long. When he was seriously discussing a particular problem in one of our drawings, the younger apprentices would slowly drift over to watch and admire the Master. He'd invariably start to show off for them.

His monologues in the car, as I drove him to look at job sites, brought me closest to understanding his thinking. "Now, Edgar," he'd say, "we want to get there as quickly as possible, but don't speed." I'd start out at about thirty miles per hour, creep up to forty or so, and in a little while we'd be racing along at eighty, ninety, ninety-five. As we sped along, he'd give himself over to grand soliloquies, with no eye to an audience. He'd talk about everything and everyone—I felt privileged to hear Mr. Wright in such a mood, voicing his deepest concerns.

These four pages of photographs
were taken by
Al Krescanko, as part of a series,
in the drafting room at Hillside.

11

arrived at Fallingwater in the summer of 1936, to pick up where Bob Mosher left off. He had taken the structure up to the second floor. It seemed natural to be there. We had worked on the plans, knew all about the pieces that would come together to make the building—it was half framed, anyway. Nothing to it, just see that everything was done the way Mr. Wright wanted it. No longer a pencil at the drawing board. On the site you were his voice, and I was fully occupied keeping my lack of outside field experience from becoming too evident, learning as fast as I could from the superintendent in charge. Just the way I'd learned plumbing and wiring. Also, I had to learn to make up the payroll.

Living alone on the remote site sixty miles south of Pittsburgh was deadly, especially after the workers left in the afternoon. Running up to Pittsburgh with the payroll each Thursday was my only relief. On the site, the Kaufmanns had a big barn of a house with gas heaters and walls lined with Audubon prints. "E. J." was a great client, warm and cordial, and he would arrange dinner and theater or concert tickets in Pittsburgh for me. He once offered to send down a piano to fill the idle hours. I needed to get up to Racine where the Johnson Wax Building was starting. But my first job was to see the roofs on Fallingwater.

Bob Mosher and I were the ones sent out most often to building sites. "Builders never have enough drawings," Mr. Wright often said. This was especially true for his buildings, which didn't fit into the usual mold, being simpler, more organic. And simplicity is hard! You can't cover everything up, as in traditional buildings, with molding upon molding. On site, we'd draw sketches, show how saw cuts should be made or stone fitted—it wasn't easy for a young man to instruct an older craftsman who'd been doing his craft in a certain way for many years. "Mr. Wright wants it like this," I'd say, hoping I was right.

The strain was great. I stole off to New York for occasional weekends, only to find that the lives of friends and relatives were moving in various directions strange to me—and I was becoming a Midwesterner. No place was home. Even Taliesin had become an overnight stop between projects. The next project was the Johnson Wax Building.

One weekend a group of art directors were entertained at Taliesin. Soon after, Herbert F. Johnson, president of the Johnson Wax Company in Racine, went to Chicago on business. He also hoped to find a sculptor for his new administration building. A local Racine architect had made sketches, but Johnson felt there was something wrong—and there was. The main facade had a modernistic entrance in the middle—with three niches on either side for bas-reliefs: a woman waxing a floor, a boy waxing a table, a man painting a mechanical object, and so forth. Terrible. The building was to be air-conditioned and windowless—the niches would be its only decoration.

Johnson asked the art director of his ad agency to suggest a sculptor for the niches. The art director said Johnson needed an architect not a sculptor. That was when Mr. Wright's name came up. The director had spent the preceding weekend at Taliesin. Johnson checked with a Chicago architect and got the word: Wright is the greatest, see him.

When we heard that the Johnson people were coming to interview Mr. Wright, we apprentices went to work: windows were washed, the grounds raked, floors cleaned and waxed, the vases were filled with foliage. Johnson arrived with his general manager and head advertising man. Mr. Wright showed them about, and luncheon was served elegantly. After they left, Mr. Wright announced that he had the job. What elation we felt . . . our first big, solid commercial project! A few days later we drove to Racine to meet the Johnson Wax staff and see the plant. Mr. Wright tried, in vain, to have the new building located in the country. He was trying his Broadacres theory. We had lunch at Mr. Johnson's often remodeled house on Main Street. They seemed headed for a close friendship and working relationship.

Back at Taliesin, Mr. Wright and we apprentices spent about ten days preparing the sketches—working day and night. We returned to Racine, to present the sketches to the clients—

stopping the car in front of the old building. I put the roll of plans under my arm, planning to follow Mr. Wright into the building. He took the roll from me and said, "The architect carries his own plans."

The presentation was complete. Mr. Wright explained that the entrance must be in the rear—from under a carport—people always under cover. He went on to stress that the building had been designed organically—the nature of the large space for all workers, the balcony around the interior perimeter, the air-conditioning an integral part of design (no niches required). There were no client suggestions or changes—working out of the details would come later. Mr. Wright collected a sizable retainer and promptly bought another farm adjacent to Taliesin.

Mr. Wright called upon former apprentice engineer Mendel Glickman to structure the project with Wes Peters; the York air-conditioning people were selected to design the heating and cooling systems. The building was to start as soon as possible—and it did start even though the Industrial Commission would not issue a permit. Mr. Wright refused to stop his progress. When asked how he could start construction without a permit, he said, "We will construct until they call out the militia." The Commission could not accept the column capabilities, so Mr. Wright had a column poured and tested. We witnessed the testing of the

Racine, Wisconsin, auspicious occasion—author with camera in hand, watching, snapping. *Left:* Contractor checking load. *Center:* Johnson manager and Mrs. Wright's daughter Svetlana. *Right:* Props removed, column toppling.

Radical Calyx column—it held thrice the required load; Mr. Wright directed the toppling. By then the building's foundations were in, the column forms made, and materials were being ordered. Finally we got the permit. Mr. Wright had conviction and courage. Johnson also had courage.

During the winter of 1937, Mr. Johnson provided us with office and living quarters behind a defunct bar-and-grill building on a corner across the street from construction. The builder, a local friend of the Johnson people who had trained as an architect, was a supreme find. He interpreted Mr. Wright's drawings faithfully—on a cost-plus basis. There were six drafting tables. I was clerk-of-the-works, and the builder also hired me a drafts-

Above: Inspecting toppled column; the impact had broken a drain line ten feet below grade.

Top right: Same day, Herbert F. Johnson and Mr. Wright.

Middle right: Wes Peters, Mr. Wright, and Mr. Johnson.

Bottom right: Ben Wiltschek, builder, and Mr. Wright.

man. I lived "in back of the store," camping out and staying close, spending weekends at Taliesin or in Chicago, an hour away. Mr. Wright wanted the apprentices back at Taliesin most weekends, presumably to report on the job. Perhaps also because he liked to keep an eye on us—he didn't like to have us off somewhere, out of sight.

Mr. Wright went to Arizona for an extended stay, and this was Mr. Johnson's written comment in the Racine drafting room, "in back of the store."

Mr. Wright was still accepting lecture engagements. Earlier his lecturing was literally necessary—to bring in funds for food. Now it provided luxuries. Upon return from an engagement, he would stop in town and purchase provisions far beyond what we needed. Once he bought out the stock of a fire sale. The crackers tasted burnt and we quietly disposed of them—he thought they tasted just fine.

As the years went on, we took most of his lectures for granted, but I remember one in particular. I was driving Mr. Wright and *New Yorker* writer Alexander Woollcott, his close friend, to Milwaukee. Woollcott, who had spent a weekend at Taliesin, was being driven to Chicago—via a Wright lecture and a look-see at Racine. Sitting with Woollcott in the back seat of the Cherokee Red Zephyr (trading up now—later it would be Continentals), Mr. Wright started defining culture with a capital "C." He began criticizing the college system (for Woollcott was a trustee of Hamilton College), saying that all colleges teach is worn-out European rot—some in a more snobbish way than others, especially Harvard, which has its own accent. It was a well-structured lecture, and Mr. Wright went on and on, becoming hotter and hotter. Poor Woollcott couldn't get a word in. Occasionally, Mr. Wright became distracted by the craft architecture of the Wisconsin indigenous red barns we were passing—only to return to his anti-college theme.

Arriving in Milwaukee, at his scheduled lecture, Mr. Wright was tired and limp—the convention group got twenty minutes of ramble. Then on toward Racine for other events. We had driven down on back roads—for the license plates had expired—but now came the real thing, city driving. We were stopped in Racine by a policeman, for speeding down main street and failing to signal at a turn. We found no registration, and my driver's license had been left in workclothes. Mr. Wright and Woollcott handled the situation together. Complimenting each other extravagantly, they put on a show that overwhelmed the officer, who soon found out he was in the presence of two great

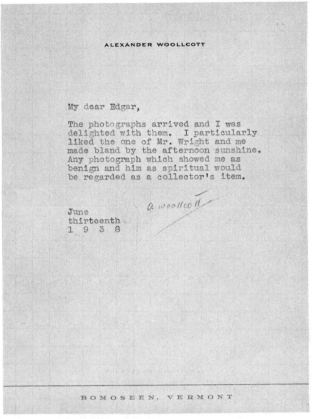

ALEXANDER WOOLLCOTT

My dear Edgar,

The photographs arrived and I was delighted with them. I particularly liked the one of Mr. Wright and me made bland by the afternoon sunshine. Any photograph which showed me as benign and him as spiritual would be regarded as a collector's item.

June
thirteenth
1 9 3 8

a. woollcott

BOMOSEEN, VERMONT

Alexander Woollcott and Mr. Wright after lunch during the Woollcott visit to Taliesin.

Americans. "Officer," declared Mr. Wright, "this is Alex Woollcott, the great *New Yorker* writer." Woollcott took his turn. "And officer, this is Wisconsin's Frank Lloyd Wright, America's foremost architect, no, the world's best architect." Interrupting each other, they bantered back and forth until the policeman was completely confused. We were excused. We got back in the car. Roared Mr. Wright, "Drive on!" I drove on.

Mr. Wright loved to show his buildings to his friend, so we drove further into Racine to see the Johnson Wax Building, still under construction. Mr. Wright got out of the car, straightened his cape, nodded to his friend, and started walking toward the building. Woollcott followed. Any moving group became a Wright procession: He was always at the head, his cane a mace. When Woollcott, who was short and heavy, caught up—inside—he looked around, felt the extraordinary presence of the building, and waved his arms, exclaiming, "Frank, I want to dance! I want to dance!" "Alex," said Mr. Wright, "*This* is education! *This* is culture!"

Sometime later, Mr. Wright told us about meeting Woollcott on a train ride from Los Angeles to New York. Mr. Wright said they'd had a fine time reminiscing at first. The next morning, at breakfast, Mr. Wright had insisted on having his bread toasted on one side only. He sent back the two-sided toast, which embarrassed Woollcott. Mr. Wright said he would not eat two-sided toast and that anyone who did was uncultured and that he, Woollcott, was displaying a lack of culture. Their parting was not cordial, according to Mr. Wright. After telling the story, Mr. Wright went into the vault and returned with the fifty-three stations of Tokaido, by Hiroshige—had them boxed handsomely and sent off to his friend. "I wouldn't want Alex to be mad at me . . ." and Alex wasn't. Several days later a long thank-you telegram came—*New Yorker* style, written for posterity. We listened to that story often again.

On the Johnson project, I was constantly traveling about, checking the progress of materials—always special—being fabricated in various shops: trips to the revolving door people (Mr. Wright invented thin revolving door rails), to Corning for glass tubing. Mr. Wright had devised a new system of glazing for the continuous-band openings to let in light—Pyrex glass tubes wired to scalloped aluminum racks, mastic between. The carpenters' union insisted that tubing was their work, the glaziers were convinced it was theirs, and even the plumbers staked a claim because the Pyrex was in the form of pipes. The carpenters prevailed and, in general, the project proceeded.

Mr. Wright blew up if we suggested that materials might not behave as he wanted them to. We thought that the glass tubing in the skylights and bands might present weather problems. Mr. Wright was determined to make the tubes work, but

Short columns engaged in carport wall, Johnson Wax Building.

"Breather," up to second floor. Mr. Wright dubbed this a "nostril."

Opening for circular elevator, and circular center core "breather."

Flare, or top of column, during pouring.

In three-story entrance, brick opening for speaker grill.

Formwork for column cap, or top.

View of glazed skylights.

Skylight being glazed with Pyrex tubing.

The great space, columns poured, floor unfinished.

View from water tower: mixing plant, center, from which concrete was pumped.

Near completion, scaffolding for installation of Pyrex tubing glass cornice.

Horse-drawn milk wagon delivering in Racine.

Years later, laboratory tower in construction.

Bronze elevator cage—elevator exposed for two floors.

the contractor—and some of us—thought there should be flat glass on the top surfaces. We could imagine the problems that might come later. I had become accustomed to supervising construction and dealing with contractors, so I got prices on flat skylights for the whole building and compared them to the cost of glass tubing, assuming I was doing the right thing. Mr. Johnson heard of the problem from the contractor and instructed him to order the flat glass and forget about the Pyrex tubes. Meanwhile, I asked Mr. Wright if he'd consider the contractor's suggestion as an alternative. He became furious. I knew he would. "If the tubes are valid in one place, they're valid all over the building." The flat skylights were being ordered, and I had to telephone Mr. Wright to tell him of the owner's change. I was right in the middle. When Mr. Johnson learned that I'd told Mr. Wright he was responsible for the order, *he* was furious; he fired me on the spot and told me to get off the premises. There was nothing else to do. I called Mr. Wright—not available. I drove on to Milwaukee, called again, and explained what had just happened. He said, "If Mr. Johnson fires you, he's firing his architect. Go back to Racine." Back I went. Johnson backed down.

Mr. Wright had told Johnson the glass tubing would be $36,000. The Corning price, when it came in, was over $70,000. Mr. Wright met the Corning president in New York and persuaded him to lower the price to $36,000, saying "It is a landmark building." The tubes leaked.

What to do about the hardware? "Schlage will furnish it." Schlage did. Furniture? "I will design it." He did. We went

View east from under continuous balcony.

to all the Johnson officials and heads of departments, obtained their requirements, and designed accordingly. No problems. Who would make the furniture? MacArthur. And MacArthur did. Mr. Wright was delegating responsibilities right and left—and continuing to look for new fields to delegate.

As costs rose, Johnson said, "At first, Mr. Wright was working for me. Then we were working together. From now on I'm working for him." Upon completion, the building became a national phenomenon. There was nothing like it anywhere. The Johnson people worked out the publicity, with Mr. Wright's help. Mr. Johnson said that during its first year the $750,000 building brought in $5 million in publicity. And Johnson's wax sold like hotcakes.

The Johnson building is the classic of our time. In plan, it is on a 20′ grid, divided into 5′ or 4′ modules, divisible by 16″. Vertically, the 3″ high brick plus ½″ joint is the module—all dimensions worked to these units of measure. Mr. Wright himself laid out the dimensions and scale. Form and function are one—the nature of materials is everywhere in presence—and very few types of material are needed to do the work. Each part subservient to the whole, yet each complete in its own right. Genius knew what, where, and when to apply itself, all for the dimension—the human scale and use. Free of small cubicles, the workspace is a forest in which to work, perform, move, and be. With each visit one feels the quality more; the user is part of this quality—its message, a way of life. The Johnson building: Mr. Wright's ninth symphony!

Mr. Wright describing his building.

In another series of Al Krescanko photographs, Mr. Wright is shown discussing the Johnson Wax Building with his client, some twenty years after completion.

When the building was almost completed, Johnson engaged Mr. Wright to design a house—"Wingspread," north of Racine on a pond in farmland. It was for himself, his wife, and their four children—four wings, emanating from a central living room forty feet by sixty feet. The basic scheme came from a Johnson sketch. Mr. Wright made it into an integral whole. Same builder, same brick—rambling and spacious, finally given to a foundation for public use.

"Wingspread" in construction.

Modern widow's walk, overlooking private airstrip.

Head of David by Mr. Wright's friend Carl Milles,
at entrance gate, on approval.
Mr. Johnson did not purchase it.

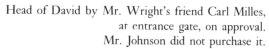

Carpenter nailing three-member cypress
cornice in place.   The two lower members
would face trellises.

Right: Mr. Wright and contractor during inspection.

Johnson was the ideal client: Mr. Wright designed everything: house, furnishings, landscaping.   Wingspread is calm,
serene, handsome, yet modest.   Mr. Johnson said he hated to
leave his home in the morning and hated to leave his office
building at the end of the day.   After World War II, Mr. Wright
went on to design a laboratory tower for the company and a
school near Wingspread.   Client's and architect's hearts seemed
always to be beating together.

After Wingspread, a Chicago newspaper editor, Lloyd Lewis, engaged Mr. Wright to design a house on the Des Plains River north of Chicago in Libertyville. They were good friends. Mr. Wright tried out another floor heating idea. Since the house was perched up high to get the view, the pipes had to go through two layers of joists. Somehow it worked, but it taxed everyone's ingenuity. Mr. Wright also submitted a budget that was impossibly low—I bid every little part of the house separately, down to hardware, clean-up, grading. There was one fight. The balcony parapet was so high that while seated Lewis couldn't see the river he liked so well. He ranted and raged; Mr. Wright said the balcony was designed correctly; they both held ground. One day, Mr. Wright suddenly issued instructions: "Cut the parapet down one board. Lloyd deserves what he wants." Lewis' friends came from the world of sports and theater—a motley group to Mr. Wright. He said, "Even Lloyd's friends look distinguished in my design."

In 1938, *Life* Magazine ran a story featuring Mr. Wright's ideas about a house for a family with an income of $5000-6000. Bernard Schwartz, of northern Wisconsin's Two Rivers, was interested in building the house on a little site. Enough land was obtained and a two-story Usonian house was developed. The living room had a long clerestory of some thirty feet; the carport was cantilevered deeply; the three-inch walls were skimpy—so

EDGAR A. TAFEL:1000 SIXTEENTH STREET:RACINE:WISCONSIN

Edgar - Go looking for an acre or two on which Schwarz could build. Feel it a shame to let him get stuck on a little urban lot?

Sincerely,
Frank Lloyd Wright
T A L I E S I N
PHOENIX:ARIZONA
January 22nd, 1939

steel beams were added without Mr. Wright's knowledge (he was busy with other matters). Schwartz questioned the bills for steel. He was not happy with the extra charges; I explained them as due to minor job conditions.

Therefore, when an apprentice went south—soon after this—to supervise a similar house, Wes and I took him aside and gave him the facts of structural life. "Tuck steel away thusly and nobody will know . . . " The apprentice was chicken; he followed the original plans. When the props came down, so did the roof. The client called Mr. Wright, whose response was "Send the boy back to Taliesin." Returning to the fold would solve everything. Mr. Wright had the plans brought out and inspected the structure. I admitted adding the steel in the Schwartz house. "I can deal with my enemies, but cannot trust my own apprentices . . . You have violated my trust. . . . This is the end. You had better start packing. First, drive me and Mrs. Wright to Madison . . . " Only a few miles out, still fuming about the betrayal, he ordered me to stop at a filling station. While he was out of the car, Mrs. Wright asked how I could do such a thing after all the years together. I pointed out that we had saved Mr. Wright's reputation in Wisconsin and that if it had to be lost by an uninformed or unseasoned apprentice, better it should happen far away—in the South. When Mr. Wright returned to the car, Mrs. Wright implored him to look at the situation differently. After all, Edgar was doing his best. The whole subject was dropped and forgotten.

Part of Schwartz house dining-living area, showing jigsawn wood and glass clerestory windows.

Below: Mr. Wright "softens" construction photograph with penciled foliage.

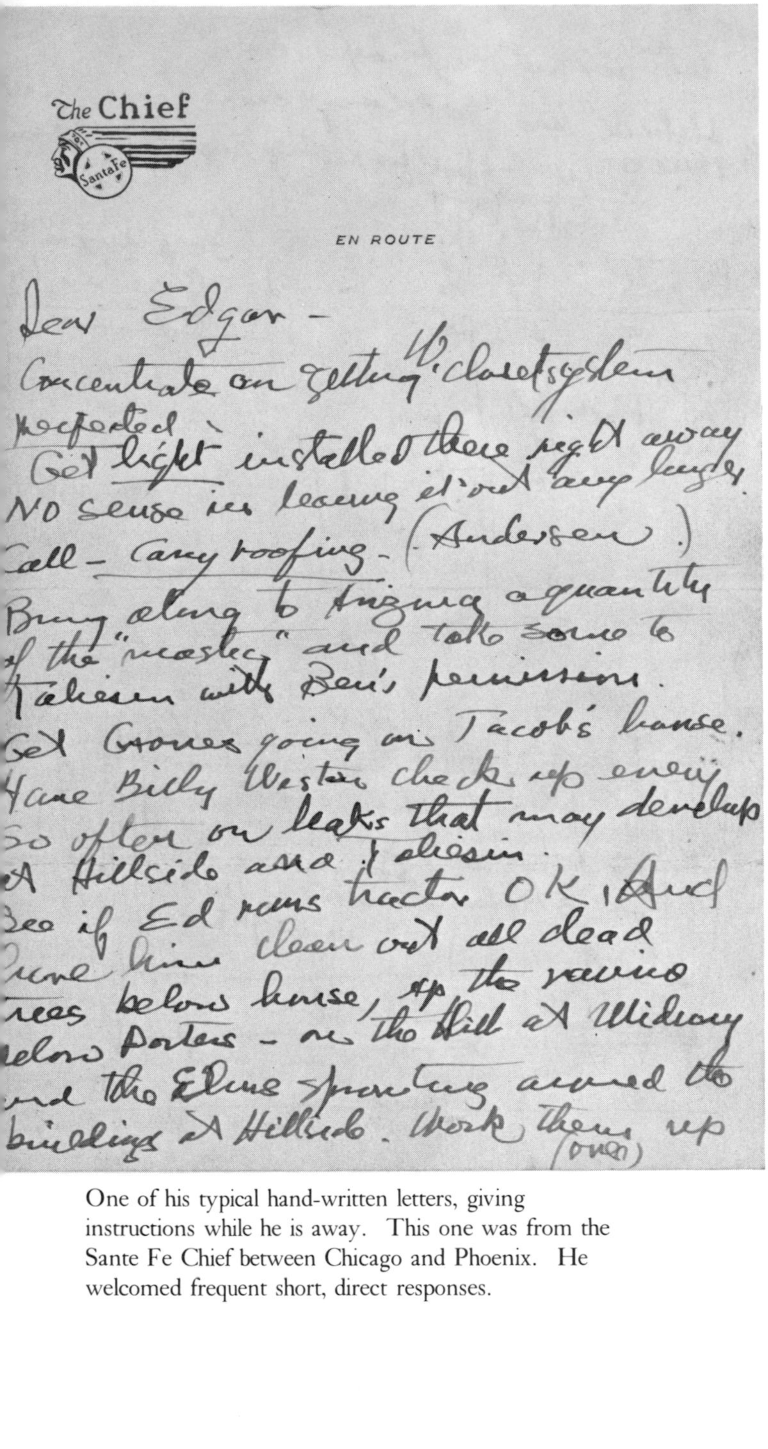

EN ROUTE

Dear Edgar —

[handwritten letter, largely illegible]

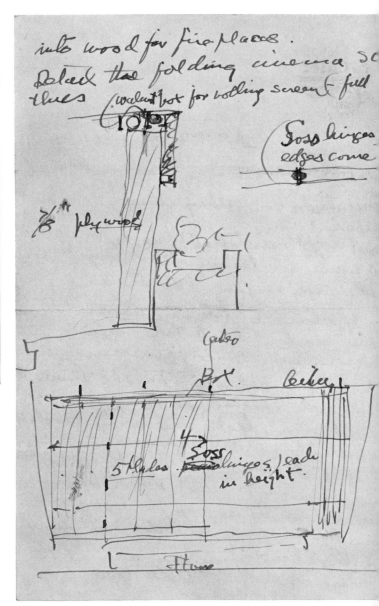

One of his typical hand-written letters, giving
instructions while he is away. This one was from the
Sante Fe Chief between Chicago and Phoenix. He
welcomed frequent short, direct responses.

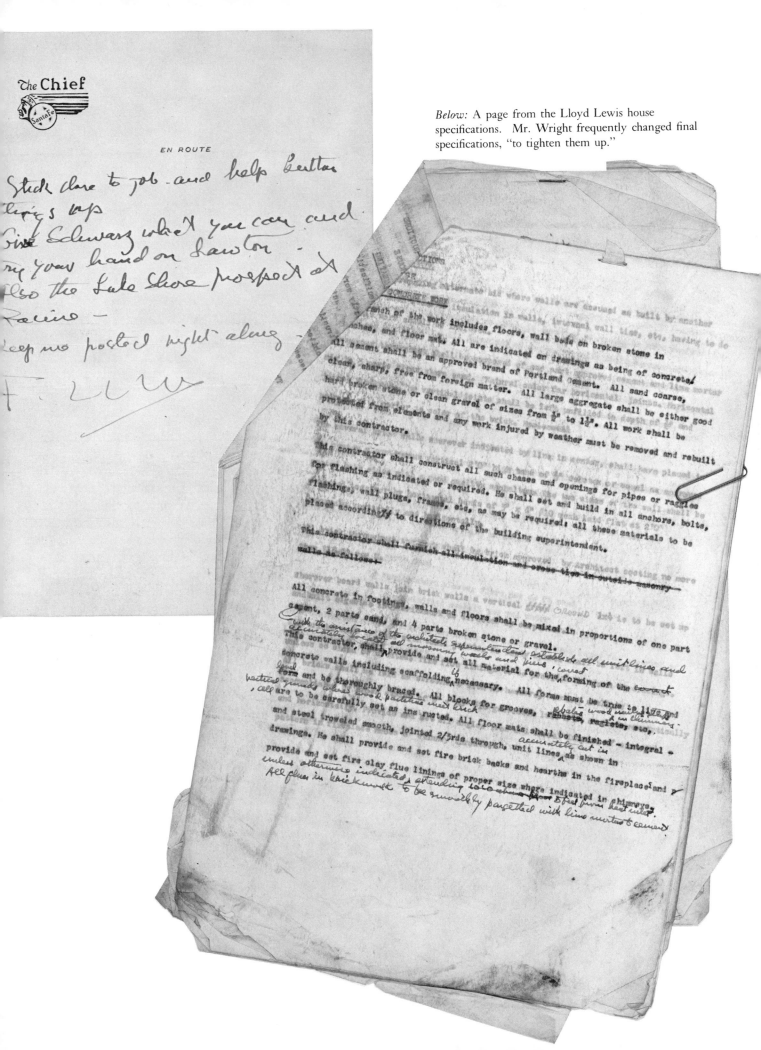

Below: A page from the Lloyd Lewis house specifications. Mr. Wright frequently changed final specifications, "to tighten them up."

The Chief
Santafe

EN ROUTE

Stick close to job - and help button
things up
Give Schwarz what you can and
try your hand on Lawton -
also the Lake Shore prospect at
Racine -

Keep me posted right along -

F. LL W

CONCRETE WORK

This branch of the work includes floors, wall beds on broken stone in arches, and floor mats. All are indicated on drawings as being of concrete.

All cement shall be an approved brand of Portland Cement. All sand coarse, clean, sharp, free from foreign matter. All large aggregate shall be either good hard broken stone or clean gravel of sizes from ¾" to 1½". All work shall be protected from elements and any work injured by weather must be removed and rebuilt by this contractor.

This contractor shall construct all such chases and openings for pipes or raggles for flashing as indicated or required. He shall set and build in all anchors, bolts, flashings, wall plugs, frames, etc, as may be required; all these materials to be placed accordingly to directions of the building superintendent.

This contractor shall furnish all insulation and cross ties in outside masonry walls as follows:

All concrete in footings, walls and floors shall be mixed in proportions of one part cement, 2 parts sand and 4 parts broken stone or gravel.

This contractor shall provide and set all material for the forming of the concrete walls including scaffolding if necessary. All forms must be true to lines and be thoroughly braced. All blocks for grooves, rabbets, register, etc, cell are to be carefully set as instructed. All floor mats shall be finished - integral - and steel troweled smooth, jointed 2/3rds through, unit lines accurately cut in drawings. He shall provide and set fire brick backs and hearths in the fireplaces and provide and set fire clay flue linings of proper size where indicated in chimneys, unless otherwise indicated, extending into chimneys. All flues in brickwork to be smoothly pargetted with lime mortar & cement

12

Arizona 1937: After two winters at the borrowed Arizona quarters called La Hacienda, a pseudo-rancho complex, Mr. Wright responded to a desire to have his own winter quarters in the desert. He well remembered his winter in the Ocatilla camp in 1928 and could no longer bear to live in another's design. He sought, found, and purchased some land, with no history of water, on a southern slope fifteen miles from Scottsdale—just sand, stones, and assorted cacti. At $3.50 per acre he felt he couldn't go wrong—he knew Arizona had a future.

A well driller named Lovelace was employed, and Mr. Wright returned to Wisconsin to await results. Telegraphs from Lovelace arrived every few days, indicating no water. Mr. Wright wired back: "Keep drilling." Finally, about $10,000 later, Lovelace wired success—which meant good-bye to La Hacienda.

That fall the Fellowship traveled again to Arizona—this time to pitch tents, set up such temporary structures as wood framework with canvas roofs. Mr. Wright called his own cabin the "Suntrap." Electricity came via a portable Kohler plant, there was a primitive septic system, there were no phones.

Mr. Wright soon devised a master plan for the camp, decided on a grammar of building, and was off to a new design concept indigenous to Arizona. Desert stone was placed in forms with a lean mortar mix. Redwood—rough-sawn, undried, and stained dark brown—was inexpensive and handsome against the white canvas roofs and the sky. Although the redwood had a strong appearance, the climate made it shrink in all directions; it twisted and even exuded nails. Eventually, years later, the wood was replaced with painted steel, in his favorite Indian color—Cherokee Red.

During the first winter new situations arose constantly. Rattlesnakes appeared with warmer weather, walls of water rolled down the washes at each heavy rain. The Wrights kept their spirits high, and the apprentices tagged along. In Arizona it can be cold in the morning, hot when the sun is high—there can be cold and wet days and nights.

Mr. Wright actually designed the camp on the site where it was being built. The apprentices were the surveyors, laying out the lines for the buildings. Drafting tables were set out in the sun, in the blazing light—imagine drafting on white paper in the Arizona sun!

Daily routine was similar to that of Taliesin, but we seemed to enjoy going to Phoenix though it offered little culturally. Mr. Wright often took several of us along on his buying expeditions and one time walked three of us into a Western clothing store. A Pendleton woolen suit, Eisenhower-type jacket with slash pockets, took his fancy. He had us fitted out, took out a fistful of bills, and paid the cashier on the spot. He wanted us to

Mr. Wright talking to Wes and Bob.

Mr. Wright, at head of table, lunching with apprentices in temporary canvas-and-wood quarters.

Mr. Wright and former apprentice Fred Langhorst, who was visiting us in Arizona.

195

look Western. Back in Chicago on a visit one day, Mr. Wright stopped in to see the owner of Fisher record players and radios, requesting a discount. He wanted a new set for his drafting room. Mr. Fisher, impressed with Mr. Wright, told him there were only two ways of obtaining his product—either through retail purchase or as an outright gift. He offered Mr. Wright the latter—whereupon Mr. W. said he had two drafting rooms—one in Wisconsin, the other in Arizona. He then said farewell, thanking Fisher for two sets.

I came down from Racine for short visits when Johnson Building problems arose and I needed direct decisions. Mr. Wright hated answering long, detailed letters, so I convinced Mr. Johnson that quick trips by air could bring ready decisions—and they did. Mr. Wright would sometimes say that I looked pale, that I needed a few days of Arizona sunshine, which meant shoveling concrete or doing carpentry in the sun—if there was sun.

For sculpture at the terminals of the walls, Mr. Wright had us bring down large rocks (decorated with petroglyphs) from the mountainside and set them in a natural-looking orientation. "When the Indians come back 2000 years from now to claim their land, they will note we had respect for their orientation." Taliesin West would make one of the most interesting ruins of all time.

Top: First blocked-out perspective of entire complex.

Middle: Views of Mr. Wright's temporary cabin, which he called the "suntrap."

Bottom: First office, temporary, with pole and flag.

Fellowship on trek back to Wisconsin, stopping at Tuba Trading Post Company on an Indian reservation for fuel and groceries.

Apprentices were divided between their love for Taliesin East and Taliesin West—many feeling that the West was the new frontier, where new ways of life would emerge, that there would be new opportunities for Mr. Wright such as he could never have back East, where his reputation had been affected by his life story. The architect goes where the work is.

The desert camp was for everyone a considerable change from the drab Wisconsin winters. The car caravan voyages from Wisconsin to the desert were generally as direct and rapid as possible. On the return, after Easter, the travelers took more creative routes—each one different—via the Grand Canyon, or Bryce Canyon, or up through Goldfield and Tonapah, Nevada. Mr. Wright was not one to choose the same route twice. We slept outdoors in sleeping bags, weather permitting, and many of our meals were like picnics. We traveled as fast as we could, despite breakdowns, flat tires, and other mishaps.

The last trip I experienced was for apprentices alone—maybe he felt we had finally grown up. Anyway, Mr. Wright put me in charge and, with about half enough money, we started the tour. For a change, the Wrights took the train. Halfway back I wired for more funds and found the money waiting at the appointed stop.

Apparently apprentices who arrived at Taliesin West (there had been previous tries at names that wouldn't stick, such as

Dear Trucketeers
We are going so well —
(hoping you are the same) that we
are pushing on to St George
132 miles —
Come on along if you can and
as soon as you can.
We will be waiting for you at
the principal hotel —
On coming through for the 188 miles
from Goldfield was just under three
hours.

F─── ──────

"Aladdin" and "Rockledge") had a different view of Fellowship life from those of us who were Wisconsin oriented. Scottsdale, only fifteen miles away, grew from a few stores to tens, and the restaurants grew from none to dozens. There was festivity in the air rather than the Spring Green farming center drabness. The land of cowboys and Indians had a festive air, and Mr. Wright took to buying Navajo rugs and artifacts.

Mr. Wright was also a collector of people. On a trip to New York City, he once met a pianist whom he invited to Taliesin West for the entire summer. He would accept a poet as an apprentice—or an artist or a weaver—to round out the kinds of people aboard. Occasionally there was a photographer in resi-

Mr. Wright enjoyed viewing and purchasing Indian rugs. Occasionally a dealer from a trading post would stop by to sell us Indian rugs.

dence. Pedro Guerrero wandered into the Desert Camp (our first name for Taliesin West), showed Mr. Wright his wares, and was immediately accepted. His father had been a house painter on the original Ocatilla camp in the desert. For several years, until World War II, Pedro photographed everything in sight—often under Mr. Wright's direction.

One day word came that the *Architectural Forum* was about to run photos of David Wright's house in Phoenix. The pictures had been taken shortly after construction, when the house didn't seem to tie to the ground. Mr. Wright later had a wall built, to "anchor," the round building to the ground. He told the *Forum* to send Pedro out to get a proper picture of the house—and its anchor. Guerrero flew to Phoenix, took one picture, and flew back to New York. His photo ran in the magazine, and the house looked fine, anchor and all.

Top left: Another rock with petroglyphs used as sculpture.

Left: Interior of living room.

Above: Drafting room.

Right: Marker at highway, metal painted Cherokee red.

Below, left to right: Square tile glazed red, signature FLLW; glass cut to fit around bowl; memento sculpture to Svetlana Peters—three plow discs forming a birdbath.

13

During the Johnson Wax Building construction I was asked to describe Mr. Wright's concepts at a luncheon for businesspeople. An attorney in the audience came up later to introduce himself. He'd just bought the Hardy House (1905). I suggested that he and his family move into the house right away, after painting it neutral off-white. Mr. Wright, who was off on a trip to Russia, would want them to start out that way. No fee was accepted—Taliesin was an ongoing service.

When one of the attorney's employees was looking for an architect, I was suggested. My career started with a bang, a big house right on Lake Michigan! My designing was helped by Mr. Wright's constant suggestions. He could look at a problem and immediately see a solution. Later, Mr. Wright heard that "Edgar's house was great—within time and under budget." Praise for an apprentice? Nothing could be worse! The house was leading to other commissions that would be done under the Taliesin umbrella, and I was delighted. Wasn't this what it was all about?

With one house under my belt, I was able to get married—to a Madison graduate in the arts. During our honeymoon, in the East, Wes called: A house in Amherst, Massachusetts, was in trouble—would I stop there and help? Of course I would. The floor heating pipes had frozen, subcontractors had fled, funds were needed for completion, there was a fire, the client was

Thomas P. Hardy house, Racine, Wisconsin, 1905.
Below: View from lakeside; drawing from Wasmuth
edition of Wright's work, 1910.

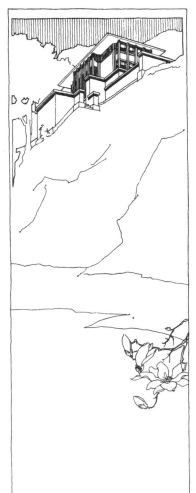

distraught, same old thing. Our honeymoon was a series of New England boiled dinners. Then we went back to Taliesin where the dam had broken, the roads were flooded, and the farmer had gone off without waiting for a replacement. Everything was fouled up—as usual. For the rest of the winter we tried adapting to the various situations, preparing for the Fellowship's return from Arizona.

Other Racine architectural prospects were in sight for me: a store and several houses. Mr. Wright saw the problem. Naturally, the apprentice would want to tend to his own work first. Mr. Wright wanted apprentices to attend to Wright projects first. The air was strained. I brought in another house and began sketches in the usual manner, working them up and bringing them to Mr. Wright for comment and approval before showing them to the client.

Soon, one evening, Mr. Wright called a general meeting of the Fellowship. He had never done this before, except for a talk after dinner or to meet a dignitary. Something was up. The purpose of the meeting, it turned out, was to make it clear that from now on there would be only one architect at Taliesin, Mr. Wright himself. We could not work directly for clients, for that would confuse the general direction at Taliesin. An apprentice could bring in work, he would be in charge of the project, and the fee would be divided—two-thirds would go to the Fellowship. Previously, the sharing had been fifty-fifty. The change seemed not to be a problem to the other apprentices, for only two of us had brought in work. Mr. Wright was to be the sole designer. Would it work?

With financial support coming only from outside work, with dentist bills and clothes to buy, the problem was survival. Mr. Wright took on my new client, they worked together, the fee was not distributed. One day I stopped in the office and complained that things weren't working out.

Mr. Wright said, "Give it a chance." He reached into his pocket, pulled out a hundred dollar bill, and handed it over. That didn't seem right, but I decided to give it a chance. Mr. Wright had changed courses before. He might change again.

The situation grew worse. We seniors had our positions as principals taken away—gloom set in on several fronts. There were war clouds that summer of 1941. Mr. Wright hated the

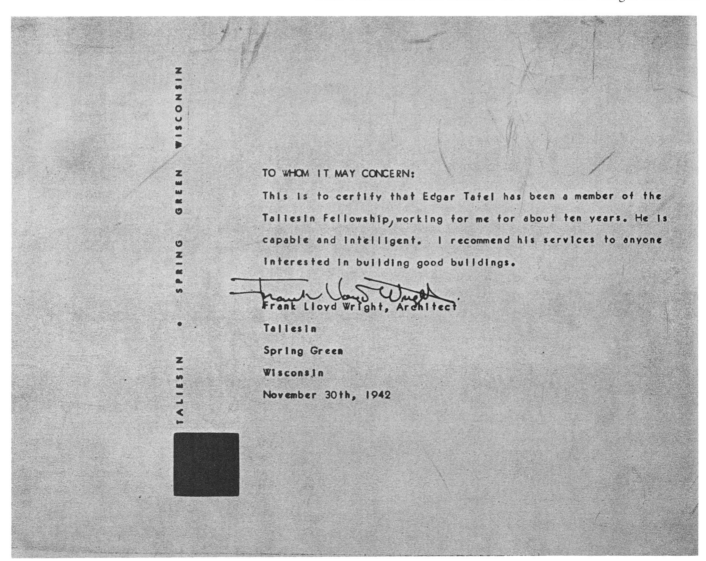

TALIESIN • SPRING GREEN WISCONSIN

TO WHOM IT MAY CONCERN:

This is to certify that Edgar Tafel has been a member of the Taliesin Fellowship, working for me for about ten years. He is capable and intelligent. I recommend his services to anyone interested in building good buildings.

Frank Lloyd Wright, Architect

Taliesin

Spring Green

Wisconsin

November 30th, 1942

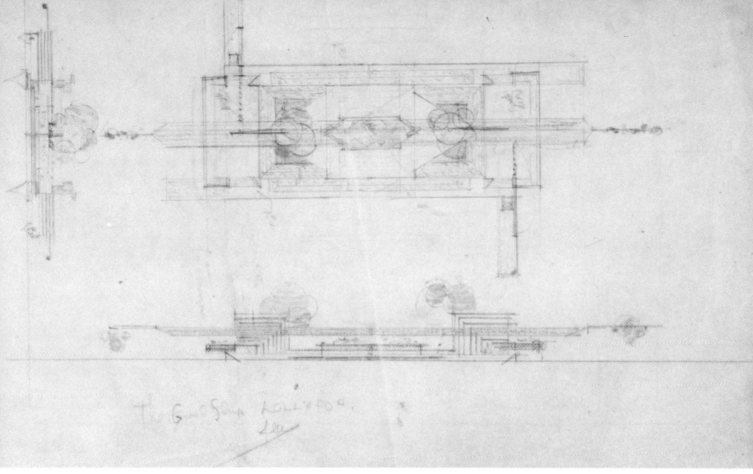

The only original drawing I have of Mr. Wright's. He was rummaging through a drawer, pulled this one out, crumpled it and threw it on the floor. I asked him if I might have it and he said, "Take it." It has been a companion ever since.

idea of war. War never settled anything, let the world stew, he said. We had to register for the draft. We felt it was other peoples' war.

One night a group of us "oldsters," all under thirty, were sitting around drinking beer, turning over our problems. The more we talked the worse everything seemed. Suddenly I said, "I can't stay. I'm leaving." My statement was like a bombshell. Others decided to leave also. We agreed, though, that the exodus would not be in protest. There were seven of us. We planned to leave one by one and did.

Early the next morning I went to Mr. Wright's office. "Good morning, sir," I said. "I've given the new system a chance and I don't think it will work. I'm leaving."

Mr. Wright looked at me. "Since you know what you want to do," he said, "the sooner the better. Tell Mrs. Wright your decision."

I went into the house and told Mrs. Wright that I'd definitely made up my mind: "I'm leaving today." We both shed tears. After nine years, I left between breakfast and dinner. She was gracious and I'm sure she understood: I had grown up.

If I hadn't left then, it would certainly have been later— better sadness now than frustration and a bitter separation later on. Mr. Wright was running his own office. He always would be. He was an architect first.

EPILOG

M r. Wright had taken an apartment in the Plaza Hotel, New York City. It was convenient, the best of its kind, and elegant—for he decorated it. From the Plaza, on his trips to New York, he would be able to reach the Guggenheim easily when it went into construction, and he could entertain elegantly there. Upon arriving in the city he used to call friends, clients, and editors, inviting them to breakfast or tea. The invitation was for an *intime* visit, but in the end there might be a few couples or twenty people. He enjoyed the theater, seeing old friends and meeting new people, appearing on radio and television. At one tea, held in the Palm Room of the Plaza—there were too many for the suite—he asked what we would like: iced tea, coffee, cookies? When the waiter came to him, last, he said, "As for me, I'll have a double Bushmills."

Solomon Guggenheim, sponsor of the museum, was no ordinary man and, like so many of outstanding personalities who engaged the master, he became no ordinary client. Guggenheim also had an apartment in the Plaza and, when the spirit moved, Mr. Wright would show friends Guggenheim's paintings, hung like paintings in nineteenth-century galleries—from baseboard to ceiling. They would go into the museum collection.

To Mr. Wright, I was still that boy from New York. Occasionally he telephoned and I would hear his voice, after a clearing of the throat. "Edgar, it is Saturday. Can you get some drawings blueprinted?" We apprentices never advanced beyond the age at which he'd first met us.

Mr. Wright was introduced to nonobjective art by Guggenheim's close friend, art collector Hilla Rebay. They had started a small museum off Fifth Avenue just below Fifty-Seventh Street in a fashionable area. Undoubtedly Rebay selected Mr. Wright as architect for the site at 89th Street and Fifth Avenue. He did not consider it the best permanent location: It was too far uptown. He really wanted his building in Central Park.

The "ramps" extended out beyond the building line by some six feet in the original scheme, so people downtown could see his building. He also came up with the idea of a circular interior ramp. Planning went on through the war years and land acquisition was slow. The city building department put up many obstacles, costs were mounting, and Guggenheim was becoming restless. At that time, Robert Moses, Mr. Wright's cousin by marriage, was a New York City commissioner of just about everything. He had a warm feeling toward Mr. Wright, though he hated the proposed building. When the chips were down, Moses called the buildings commissioner and demanded that a building permit reach his desk by the next day. He got it. Sometimes it's possible to get action in Gotham City—not often.

Meanwhile, former apprentice Bob Mosher, who was temporarily in New York, took a job with a big construction outfit. His company gave him a set of Guggenheim plans to review; the firm was to bid on the job. (Guggenheim had set $2 million as top limit.) Bob brought the plans to my office, and we pored over them. Mr. Wright had done it again—something new, fluid, a new idea in museums. While the plans were around, my client George Cohen, the owner of Euclid Contracting, came by. I had designed his new house in suburbia, using poured concrete wherever possible. George went wild with excitement: "I've got to get on the bidding list. Can you help me? Can I meet Wright?" Next time Mr. Wright was in town I told him about George, my concrete man. "He pours foundations, ramps, bridges, arches, anything concrete." "No, Edgar," Mr. Wright said, "the big companies are going to bid the job below their cost just to be able to say they have built the Guggenheim." Poor George, he wasn't even on the bidding list.

About six weeks later at 7:00 A.M. on a Saturday, my phone rang. Hearing someone clear his throat on the other end, I said "Hello, Mr. Wright. How are you?" "Battered, but still in the ring. Edgar, where's your concrete man? Get him here as soon as possible. I'm at the Plaza." The lowest bids came in at twice the budget and Mr. Wright had remembered the concrete man. I waited until a respectable 9:00 A.M. and phoned George. "Can't he wait until Monday? I have a foursome on the course this morning." "George, get yourself down to the Plaza before eleven. It's your chance." George asked "What happened?"

Edgar Kaufmann and I visited Mr. Wright at the Plaza Hotel in New York City in 1957. He took out two photographs and inscribed one for each of us: "To Edgar the Tafel—affection and hope" and "To Edgar the Kaufmann . . ."

209

"The bids came in slightly over the budget." "Oh." At 11:00 A.M. George rang Mr. Wright's doorbell. "So you are the expert in concrete?" "No, Mr. Wright, I have come to learn from you." Mr. Wright said, "You are my man." George became his man and built the building within the budget. They became fast friends. George wanted to build the museum the way Mr. Wright wanted it.

Mr. Wright didn't live to see the museum building completed. In a discussion about a cornerstone, George had asked if the name of his company—Euclid Contracting—could be on the cornerstone. "A round building doesn't have a cornerstone, George." Mr. Wright replied. "My name will be there as architect and yours as builder. When we are long gone, nobody will need to know the name of a company."

Solomon R. Guggenheim Museum, New York City, 1956.

Left: "Cornerstone"—FLLW [in red square] ARCHITECT GEORGE N. COHEN BUILDER.

Mr. Wright's last picnic, April 1959.

In April 1959, a radio announcer said, "Frank Lloyd Wright [my heart sank] died yesterday in Phoenix, Arizona. . . ." No, it couldn't be; yes, it was inevitable. My tears streamed. I thought, how sad, how tragic—why can't genius live forever? Everything seemed mundane in comparison to him. I would miss him so. He had always seemed to be somewhere, far or near, with strength and warmth. He would be no more. An era had ended.

He had been taken ill at Taliesin West and was brought to the Phoenix hospital. Two days later he died. Wes Peters and two apprentices took his body to Wisconsin for the funeral. They drove the station wagon straight through, day and night. Son Lloyd phoned Wes at Taliesin, asking that a death mask be made. Wes went to Spring Green, bought plaster of paris, made the mask himself, and sent it to Lloyd.

Many of us came, from all parts of the country, for the last moments. Mr. Wright's body was laid out in a simple open coffin next to his beloved grand piano in the living room. We moved about in silence—we couldn't believe it was real. Later the coffin was placed on a flat bed wagon, drawn by two work-horses, and the cortege moved solemnly down the back road. Family and apprentices were followed by friends and neighbors. The bell tolled from the chapel across the valley. We walked in silence. At the chapel yard, where the grave had been dug, the casket was removed to the grave. No one even whispered. The coffin was lowered. Apprentices shoveled in earth to fill the void. There would always be a void.

Taliesin revisited. Before Mr. Wright's death, Mrs. Wright planned his birthday party for June 6th, in Wisconsin. She decided not to cancel the party. These are the photographs I took on that occasion.

Wisconsin River.

Highway 23 in the valley.

Parking areas.

Lower parking court.

Chinese bronze tigers.

Looking back.

Living room chimney.

The upper court.

Living room.

Bird-watching balcony.

The valley.

Poppies by the roadside.

Fields below Taliesin.

Bridge over brook, Midway Gardens sculpture.

Mr. Wright's niece Elizabeth Gillham,
Marc Connelly, Adlai Stevenson,
Mr. Wright's sister Maginel.

Studio and Mr. Wright's office.

Looking down from the office.

Courtyard.

The tea circle.

Toward Mr. Wright's bedroom.

The loggia.

Mr. Wright's bedroom.

The studio.

The second Francis W. Little house, Deephaven, Minnesota, 1912.

Curators in living room on first visit.

Library room of Little house, as installed in Allentown Art Museum, Allentown, Pennsylvania.

Little House: Ten Wright houses have been "saved for posterity"—each house a story in its own right, each saved because of several concerned people who contributed their time and effort.

In 1971, former apprentice John Howe wrote me a letter saying that the 1914 Minneapolis Francis W. Little house was to be torn down. The local American Institute of Architects made slight efforts to save it, local museums had no mechanisms for preservation, and there seemed no real way to stave off destruction. The Stevensons (the original owner's daughter and her husband) were in their eighties and their family was dispersed. Under strict zoning, the site could accommodate several houses. Zoning did not allow for a public building. The house was enormous, much too large for two people. Demolition was scheduled, and the Stevensons were already building a small house next door.

Mrs. Little had been a musician, a student of Liszt's. She and Francis Little had specified a house designed for large summer gatherings, overlooking a lake. They had moved their furnishings from their previous 1905 Wright house in Peoria, slightly smaller in scale.

Donald Loveness, a friend of the Stevensons and a local Wright client as well as a Wright buff, obtained a "hold" of the demolition action. What to do with the house? Where should it go? Who would want it, or its parts? The moment plans were announced, would-be do-gooders would creep out of the woodwork and decry the destruction of a landmark; the press would cry rape. The house could be lost!

It seemed most logical to this New Yorker that the Metropolitan Museum of Art, then expanding its American Wing, and only half a mile from the Guggenheim, should have the great Little living room—35 feet wide by 65 feet long. It could be

used for seminars, musicals, gatherings, and would exemplify a Prairie house room. Millions of people could see it each year. Mr. Wright might not like being sandwiched between tepees and a colonial kitchen, but you can't have everything. I put in my word: save it fast. He could have his work in Central Park!

Arthur Rosenblatt, the Metropolitan's architect, and I had previously tried in vain to save parts of the Imperial Hotel. We now mulled over photographs of the Little house and thought it the ideal room. He brought the idea to director Thomas Hoving, who, fortunately, had recently seen the house. Swearing us all to secrecy, Hoving gave the word to go—go get the house. I flew out a couple of days later with two curators to start negotiations. Loveness met us at the airport, the weather was gloomy, and we were wondering if we could consummate such an arrangement. One miss and you are lost. However, when we entered the living room, with cocktails for the occasion, a genial climate of people, success seemed assured. There was a fire in the fireplace, the sun emerged and lit the atmosphere, and a curator exclaimed, "We must have this house." Mr. Wright seemed to be directing the operation from someplace beyond. We concluded an arrangement in which the library room went to the Allentown Museum extension I was designing, and we all went off in different directions—Don and I going to his Usonian house to gloat over our roles in a coup. As in most theatrical successes, each participant felt like the star of the drama.

Later the Stevensons had a farewell party for the house. We joined their relatives and friends of three generations. Saving the Little house required no public meetings, committees, groups, politicians, preservationists, historians, planners, or architects' societies—just a few of us with hearts in the right place and with the financial ability to act.

Full view of living room.

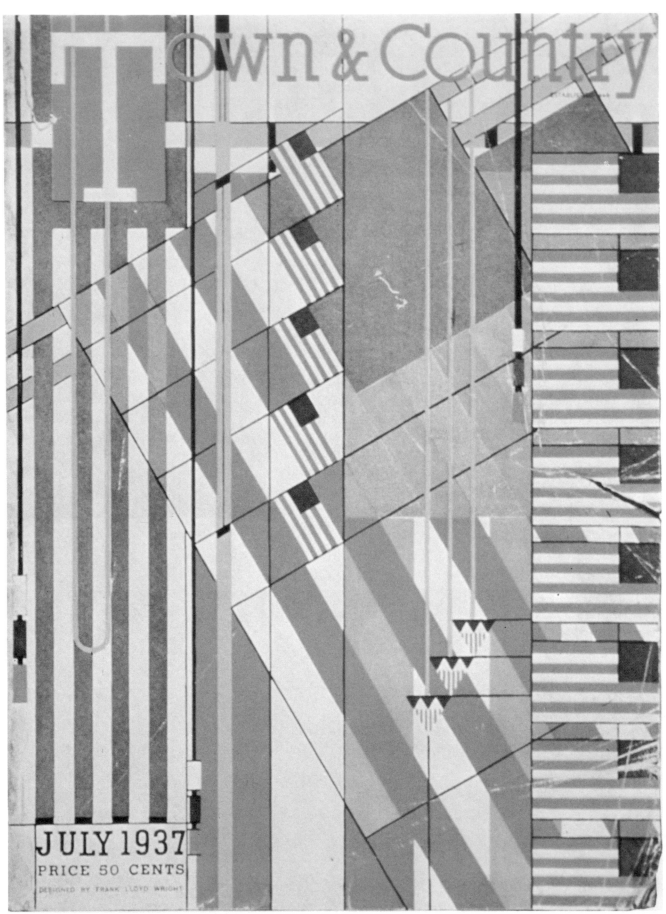

Frank Lloyd Wright's design for the front cover of the
July 1937 issue of *Town & Country* Magazine.

CREDITS

By permission of *Town & Country,* Hearst Publications, and courtesy of Nora Natof and the Smithsonian Institution's Renwick Gallery 218
The letters on pages 190, 192, 193, 198, and 199, the telegram on page 142, and the drawings on pages 97, 118, and 197 are published by permission and courtesy of the Frank Lloyd Wright Foundation, © 1979 by the Frank Lloyd Wright Foundation.

APPENDIX

Selected Frank Lloyd Wright buildings
privately owned
and
open to the public

1902   Susan Lawrence Dana residence
         301 East Lawrence Avenue
         Springfield, Illinois 62703

1904   Unity Temple
         Lake Street at Kenilworth Avenue
         Oak Park, Illinois 60302

1911   Taliesin
and Riverview Terrace Restaurant (1953)
         Route 23
         Spring Green, Wisconsin 53588

1915   A. D. German Warehouse (now Richland Museum)
         316 South Church Street
         Richland Center, Wisconsin 53581

1936   S. C. Johnson & Son Administration Building
         1525 Howe Street
         Racine, Wisconsin 53403

1937   Taliesin West
         Shea Boulevard
         Scottsdale, Arizona 85258

1938–1954   Florida Southern College
         South Johnson Avenue at Lake Hollingsworth Drive
         Lakeland, Florida 33802

1947   Unitarian Church
          900 University Bay Drive
          Shorewood Hills, Wisconsin 53704

1948   V. C. Morris Gift Shop
          140 Maiden Lane
          San Francisco, California 94108

1954   Beth Sholom Synagogue
          Old York Road at Foxcroft
          Elkins Park, Pennsylvania 19117

1955   Dallas Theater Center
          3636 Turtle Creek Boulevard
          Dallas, Texas 75219

1956   Greek Orthodox Church
          North 92d at West Congress Street
          Wauwatosa, Wisconsin 53225

1956   Solomon R. Guggenheim Museum
          Fifth Avenue at 89th Street
          New York, New York 10028

1957   Marin County Civic Center and Hall of Justice
          North San Pedro Road at U.S. 101
          San Raphael, California 94903

1959   Gammage Memorial Auditorium
          Apache Boulevard at Mill Avenue
          Tempe, Arizona 85281

Selected Frank Lloyd Wright buildings
publicly owned
and
open to the public

1893   Frank Lloyd Wright home and studio
Forest and Chicago Avenues
Oak Park, Illinois 60302

1904   D. D. Martin house
State University at Buffalo, Alumni Association
123 Jewett Avenue
Buffalo, New York 14214

1906   Frederick G. Robie house
Adlai Stevenson Center
5757 Woodlawn Avenue
Chicago, Illinois 60637

1914   Francis W. Little house ("Northome")
Note: The house was demolished; rooms were
reconstructed at:
Allentown Art Museum
5th and Court Streets
Allentown, Pennsylvania 18105
Metropolitan Museum of Art
1071 Fifth Avenue
New York, New York 10028

1917   Aline Barnsdall house ("Hollyhock House")
            4800 Hollywood Boulevard
            Los Angles, California 90027

1935   E. J. Kaufmann house ("Fallingwater")
            Western Pennsylvania Conservancy
            Mill Run, Pennsylvania 15464

1936   Paul R. Hanna house ("Honeycomb House")
            737 Frenchman's Road
            Stanford, California 94305

1937   Herbert F. Johnson house ("Wingspread")
            Johnson Foundation
            33 East 4 Mile Road
            Wind Point, Wisconsin 53402

1939   Loren Pope (Pope-Leighey house)
            Woodlawn Plantation
            Mount Vernon, Virginia 22121

1940   Gregor Affleck house
            1925 North Woodward Avenue
            Bloomfield Hills, Michigan 48013